D1084168

TWAYNE'S WORLD AUTHORS SERIES

A Survey of the World's Literature

Sylvia E. Bowman, Indiana University
GENERAL EDITOR

CHINA

William R. Schultz, University of Arizona
EDITOR

Yang Wan-li

TWAS 413

Gazing Afar Midst Cloudy Peaks, attributed to
Hsia Kuei (fl. 1190–1230), in the collection of
the Palace Museum, Peking.

YANG WAN-LI

By J. D. SCHMIDT
University of Windsor

TWAYNE PUBLISHERS
A DIVISION OF G. K. HALL & CO., BOSTON

Copyright © 1976 by G. K. Hall & Co.

All Rights Reserved

First Printing

Library of Congress Cataloging in Publication Data

Schmidt, J   D   1946–
    Yang Wan-li.

    (Twayne's world authors series; TWAS 413: China)
    Bibliography: p. 169–70.
    Includes index.
    1. Yang, Wan-li, 1127–1206.
PL2687.Y3Z87   895.114   76–18839
ISBN 0–8057–6255–8

MANUFACTURED IN THE UNITED STATES OF AMERICA

To my Mother and Father

Contents

About the Author

Preface

Chronology

1. Poet and Official   15
2. Theory of Literature   38
3. The Live Method   56
4. Illusion and Reality   78
5. The World of Man   84
6. The World of Nature   103
7. The Transcendence of Sorrow   136
8. Posterity   147

Notes and References   151

Selected Bibliography   169

Index   171

About the Author

J. D. Schmidt was born in Oak Park, Illinois in 1946. He did his undergraduate work at the University of California, Berkeley, during which period he spent two years in Taiwan studying modern and classical Chinese. Dr. Schmidt obtained his M.A. in 1970 on the poetry of Han Yü and his Ph.D. on the poetry of Yang Wan-li in 1975 from the University of British Columbia. He spent a year in India (1970–71) studying Sanskrit literature and Buddhist philosophy. Currently Dr. Schmidt is teaching in the Department of Asian Studies, University of Windsor, Ontario, Canada. He has published two articles on Sung poetry and is presently writing a book on the nineteenth century poet Huang Tsun-hsien for Twayne and a source book on Chinese literary theory from earliest times to nineteenth century.

Preface

The poetry of Yang Wan-li belongs to an age which Western historians of Chinese literature have almost totally neglected. Although a reasonable amount of material has been published concerning Chinese literature before the tenth century, literature written in the classical language after the T'ang dynasty is largely *terra incognita*. The tremendous body of writings is no doubt one of the reasons for this neglect, but the generally antiquarian interests of many scholars of classical Chinese is probably the most important factor. In spite of the widely current view that Chinese culture somehow stagnated after T'ang times, Western scholars will soon discover that the later periods of Chinese literary history are just as rich if not richer than ancient and early medieval times.

The twelfth century in which Yang Wan-li lived was one of the most productive periods in Chinese culture. In philosophy Chu Hsi was completing his synthesis of neo-Confucianism, which would exert a strong influence on Chinese thought down into modern times. The arts of Chinese painting and calligraphy had entered one of their most glorious ages, and the ceramics of the Chinese were prized and imitated from Japan to the coasts of east Africa. Poetry witnessed the perfection of a new form, the *tz'u*, and colloquial drama and short stories were gradually evolving. All of these innovations in the cultural sphere were supported by an unprecedented economic growth and a startling advance in science and technology.

Yang Wan-li's poetry did not develop in isolation from this new culture, and we have constantly striven to relate Yang's highly original verse to the innovative spirit of the age in which he was living. Although some modern critics tend to minimize the cultural milieu of an author in favor of a formalistic, analytical approach to poetry, we feel that Yang Wan-li's works are best understood in the context of the intellectual and artistic background of twelfth century China. The poet of Yang Wan-li's age was not just a poet but frequently combined his literary pursuits with an active political career, speculation in the realms of religion and philosophy, creation of works in the visual arts, and, in some cases, original research in the natural sciences or medicine.

Not only have we studied Yang Wan-li's poetry in its relationship to other cultural phenomena of his age, but our entire approach to his poetry has been deeply influenced by traditional Chinese literary criticism. The reader will find minimal use made of the tools of the modern Western literary critic, because we strongly feel that these tools are not as helpful for the study of Chinese literature as the methodology and terminology employed by critics of Yang Wan-li's own literary tradition. Thus, the reader will discover that we constantly employ the terminology of Ch'an (Zen) Buddhism to analyze Yang's works, not only because Yang was deeply influenced by that philosophy but also because most of the critics of his age utilized Ch'an language in their own writings. We have found a study of Yang's "live method" more fruitful than, say, an analysis of his poetic "imagery." Gradually the scholars of the Indian Sanskrit and the Islamic Arabic literary traditions are turning to the native critical writings to elucidate the literary products of the respective cultures, and we feel that scholars of Chinese literature must follow a similar line of research.

Anyone wishing to understand Yang Wan-li's poetry owes a great debt to the modern scholar Chou Ju-ch'ang. Although his book *Yang Wan-li hsüan-chi (Selected Writings of Yang Wan-li)* is only meant as an anthology of Yang's works for readers beginning the study of Chinese poetry, it contains a huge amount of valuable material for the serious scholar. Chou's introductory study is somewhat limited because of the ideological conflicts of modern China, but his notes for the poems selected are a model for other scholars to imitate, and we have closely followed his elucidation of obscure points relating, for example, to literary allusions and difficult language. Although we have translated many poems by Yang Wan-li not contained in Chou's anthology, his book selects most of Yang's best poetry in each major category, and, hence, many of the poems translated here also appear in Chou's work.

Since this book contains numerous translations of both Yang's poetry and critical statements concerning his work, we should say something about the method used in translating Chinese texts. Anyone who has read much classical Chinese is very familiar with the incredible difficulties of the language, and, hence, it is quite conceivable that more than one translation of a passage is correct. Generally speaking, we have attempted to translate as literally as possible without unduly distorting the English language. The reader may be somewhat surprised by the colloquial English used to translate Yang's poems, in particular, but we believe that such a style is absolutely necessary to convey the feeling that Yang Wan-li's poetry gives to the reader in the original.

I would like to express my appreciation to Professors Yeh Chia-ying, Li Ch'i, and E. G. Pulleyblank of the University of British Columbia for checking most of the translations in this book while supervising my Ph.D. dissertation. Also, I would like to thank Professor P. Demiéville for making helpful suggestions concerning translations of texts relevant to Yang Wan-li's literary theory. However, all errors of translation and interpretation are my own responsibility. In addition, I am very grateful to the Canada Council for financial assistance during the period when much of the research for this book was in progress.

J. D. Schmidt

Chronology

1127   Yang Wan-li born in Chi-shui Kiangsi province. Chinese government driven south by Chin Tartars.

1154   Yang obtains *chin-shih* degree and first official post.

1161   Meeting with Sung general Chang Chün.

1163   Unsuccessful counterattack against Chin Tartars.

1164   Yang's father dies. Three years' mourning.

1170   Yang appointed governor of Feng-hsin County.

1171   Promoted to central government in capital Hangchow.

1174   Quits post and returns home.

1178   Governor of Ch'ang-chou. Poetic "sudden enlightenment."

1179   Appointed to Kuang-tung province.

1181   Suppresses insurrection in Kuang-tung.

1182   Mother dies. Three years' mourning.

1184   Appointed to central government again.

1188   Insults emperor and is demoted to local post in Kiangsi.

1189   Recalled to central government.

1190   Clashes with emperor and demoted to local post.

1192   Retires from public service to his native village Chi-shui.

1206   Disastrous campaign against Chin. Yang dies same year at home.

CHAPTER 1

Poet and Official

I Youth in a Chaotic Period

YANG Wan-li was born in Chi-shui of modern Kiangsi province in the year 1127, the first year of the reign of the first Southern Sung emperor Kao-tsung (reg. 1127–1163). Many of the greatest poets of the Southern Sung were born at about the same time, and Yang was two years junior to Lu Yu (1125–1210) and one year junior to Fan Ch'eng-ta (1126–1193). Although Yang's family was not of peasant stock, his background was quite humble, for none of his ancestors had occupied more than the lowest local official positions.[1]

The years immediately preceding Yang's birth had witnessed political events which had a disastrous effect on the next two hundred years of Chinese history. From a relatively strong beginning under the first two emperors, the Sung dynasty had weathered a series of shocks from the Khitan Tartars who inhabited the steppes and deserts to the north of China. A prolonged struggle of party strife between reformers and conservatives had sapped the vitality of the central government. The last effective emperor on the Northern Sung throne, Hui-tsung (reg. 1101–1126), was a fine painter noted for his patronage of art and literature, but in the political sphere he was totally inept. The high taxation which court luxury necessitated was partially responsible for a series of popular uprisings, which further damaged the prestige of the imperial authority. Luckily for the Sung empire, the Khitan rule was at an equally low ebb, and the last emperor of that line was as addicted to falconry as Hui-tsung was to painting.

Into this power vacuum stepped a new Tartar race, the Jurchen, who were not yet corrupted by the arts of civilization. In 1114 they attacked the Khitan and after a resounding victory, their leader declared himself emperor of the new Chin dynasty. Upon hearing of the victory of the Chin over the Khitan, Hui-tsung was overjoyed, for now he thought that he had an ally against the old Khitan enemies. In 1120 a treaty was signed between the Sung and Chin dynasties, and both states proceeded to attack the unfortunate Khitan. By 1122 the Khitan emperor was forced from his capital, and the Sung and Chin eagerly divided up the Khitan territory. However, during the campaigns against the Khitan, the Chin generals had noticed the almost incredible ineptness of the Chinese armies, and, therefore, in 1125 the Chin launched a devastating attack against the Sung, during which they captured the Sung capital and took captive the Chinese emperor and most of his family. The Northern Sung dynasty ceased to exist, and the future of all China hung in the balance.

The Chin quickly occupied north China and set up a Chinese official as puppet emperor. Meanwhile, the ninth son of Hui-tsung ascended the imperial throne in Nanking, thereby inaugurating the Southern Sung dynasty. Although we know very little about Yang Wan-li's youth, we can be reasonably certain that the family was little troubled by the disorders of this period except indirectly from tax increases and fiscal disorder. Kiangsi lay far from the main theaters of battle, and Yang did not experience the bitterness of exile from a northern home as did the poet Hsin Ch'i-chi (1140–1207),[2] nor did he suffer the life of a wandering refugee as did Lu Yu. Lu Yu was born on the banks of the Huai River in Kiangsu province, which was one of the main battlefields, and he summed up his childhood experiences later when he wrote, "When a child, I died ten thousand times, escaping from the barbarian soldiers."[3] Although Yang Wan-li was reared in poverty, he did not suffer the trauma of warfare, which partially explains his happier outlook on life compared to many of his contemporaries.

II Early Official Career

Despite Yang's relative poverty, he was able to pursue a classical education from an early age, and in 1154, he had his first success in official life, obtaining his *chin-shih* degree in the civil service examinations at the relatively young age of twenty-eight. The poet Fan Ch'eng-ta passed in the same year, and it is quite likely that they became friends at this time. As was the custom of the age, Yang was given a position in local government soon after he passed, and his three years as Finance Inspector (*ssu-hu*) at Kan-chou were his first lengthy stay away from his family.[4] Even so, Kan-chou was not more than a hundred miles south of Chi-shui, so he could have easily gone home to visit his parents.

After the customary three years of service at Kan-chou, Yang was transferred to the post of Assistant Subprefect of Ling-ling. This was a slightly higher post but no sudden rise to fame and fortune, and now Yang was stationed far away from his family, in southwestern Hunan province. Nevertheless, the three years that Yang spent at Ling-ling were among the most significant in his political and literary career, so they deserve our full attention. The most important event in Yang's life during the year 1161 was his meeting with the famous Sung general Chang Chün (1096–1164), but before we can fully understand the impact this meeting had on Yang Wan-li, we must first review the early history of the Southern Sung and explain how Chang Chün had ended up in remote Hunan by 1161.

Although the emperor Kao-tsung had come to the throne in 1127, the Chin Tartars did not let him rest easily. Initially there was some success in recovering the lost territory of north China, but Kao-tsung soon came under the influence of officials who counseled appeasement with the enemy. The Chin took this new policy of the Sung as a sign of weakness and continued to press their attacks, driving Kao-tsung farther and farther into the south, until eventually he was forced to escape certain death by taking to the seas. Just when it seemed that the Southern Sung was about to collapse, the dynasty was saved by a series of brilliant military maneuvers carried out by a group of new generals. The most famous of them, Yüeh Fei (1003–1141), managed to hold back the enemy armies in 1133 and 1134, and finally in 1135 the now confident generals petitioned Kao-tsung to recover northern China from the barbarians.

Kao-tsung hesitated to grant their request, for he had now fallen completely under the spell of the pacifist prime minister Ch'in Kuei (1090–1155), who advised an immediate peace treaty with the Chin. Historians have speculated about the emperor's motives for holding back at this critical moment in Chinese history, but it is not unlikely that Kao-tsung did not really want to recover the north at all, for a Chinese victory would have forced the Chin to return the captive emperor, and Kao-tsung realized that two emperors could not occupy the dragon throne at the same time.

Nonetheless, Kao-tsung had need of his new generals a while longer, because widespread banditry plagued the government in the lands to the south of the Yangtze River, and the generals set

about exterminating the bandits in the hope that peace in the south
would lay the foundation for a recovery of the north. But the most
startling development was Yüeh Fei's counterattack against the
Chin which followed the anti-bandit campaign. In 1140 Yüeh Fei
pushed north defeating army after army until he finally camped
within range of the old Northern Sung capital. Yet in the same year
the pacifist Ch'in Kuei commanded Yüeh to abandon his campaign,
and in 1141 Yüeh Fei was recalled to the Southern Sung capital,
where he was murdered at Ch'in Kuei's instigation. In the same
year Ch'in Kuei encouraged Kao-tsung to submit to one of the most
humiliating treaties in Chinese history, which required the Chinese
to pay a huge indemnity to the Chin every year and recognize the
Chin state as superior to the Sung.

During the fifteen odd years of Ch'in Kuei's control of the Sung
government, most of the famous generals were eliminated and the
war party among the officials rapidly liquidated. In fact, the only
general of prominence who remained after these purges was Chang
Chün, and he was already an old man when Yang Wan-li met him in
1161. Chang had probably been spared because he was not among
the more aggressive of the Sung generals, but even so he was under
constant surveillance during the reign of Kao-tsung. When Chang
wanted to return to his native Szechwan to mourn his mother's
death, he engendered the suspicions of the pacifist party, which
forced him to be sent to Hunan province, where he could mourn his
mother but be kept safely away from his supporters in Szechwan.

When Yang Wan-li heard that such a famous man was living so
near to him, he was eager to meet Chang, for although the old
general was temporarily out of favor, he was still an influential man
and could be of use to a young, ambitious official. However, Chang
was not an easy man to visit, because he had shut his doors to all
intercourse with the outside world. In fact, Yang failed to see Chang
after three personal visits to the general's house, and only after Yang
wrote him a number of letters did Chang consent to see this young
local official. Yang was extremely impressed by the man he met, and
he held Chang Chün in higher esteem than any other statesman of
the day. During their conversation, Chang exhorted Yang to "study
with a sincere intent and upright mind," and as a result, Yang
immediately changed the name of his study to Ch'eng-chai, or Sincere Studio, and in later times he was commonly known as Yang
Ch'eng-chai.[5] In addition to encouraging Yang's studies, Chang

Chün impressed on Yang the urgency of the present political situation in China, and although we do not know anything of Yang's previous political convictions, he was henceforth firmly in the camp of those who supported strenuous resistance against the Chin Tartars.

Chang Chün exerted the greatest influence on Yang's political views at this time, but Yang's literary activities came under the influence of another friend he made while at Ling-ling, the great Southern Sung poet Hsiao Te-tsao (ca. 1147). Both Yang and Hsiao were serving in minor posts, and although Hsiao had to leave Ling-ling in 1162, Yang wrote of their friendship with great tenderness in later years. According to Yang, their very first meeting involved the writing of poetry:

I first got to know him at Ling-ling. As soon as we talked together, our minds were in accord, so I carried my bedding to his lodging, where we slept on opposite beds. At the time, the weather was hot and Hsiao wanted to set off early in the morning. He got up before me in the fifth watch, and blowing on the lamp so it flickered, he scratched his head as if occupied with something. I got up to watch him and saw he was composing a poem as a parting gift. I also wrote a poem in reply, and Hsiao was so excited he said: "Making friends is like getting engaged. Each of us has just put aside a piece of paper!"[6]

It is not certain how long Yang had been writing poetry by this time, and, alas, we shall never know, because he burned over a thousand of his earlier works in 1162, and other than a few fragments, all of his surviving poetry was composed after that date.[7] Previous to 1162 Yang had expended his poetic talents in imitating the verse of the Kiangsi school, which had formed around the Northern Sung author, Huang T'ing-chien (1045–1105). It is impossible for us to reconstruct the literary conversations of Yang and his new friend Hsiao Te-tsao, but it is very likely that Hsiao was a strong influence on Yang's eventual rejection of the artificiality of the Kiangsi poets. In later years Yang regretted having burned his youthful works, but the act was symbolic of the dramatic changes in his life during his stay in Ling-ling.

III *Disappointed Ambitions*

In 1163 the emperor Kao-tsung abdicated the throne in favor of his son, who became the next emperor Hsiao-tsung (reg. 1163–

1190). Yang must have heard the news of Kao Tsung's abdication
with high hopes, for the new emperor had a very different personality from his father. A recent victory by Chinese armies over the
Chin Tartars had encouraged Hsiao-tsung into thinking that there
was finally hope of regaining the northern half of the empire. Most
important of all, the general Chang Chün, who was now back in
favor at the imperial court, had strongly recommended Yang to the
central government, and Yang set out for the capital city immediately.

Meanwhile, plans to attack the Chin were developing apace.
Chang Chün, who had been named commander-in-chief, appointed
two generals to lead the Chinese army northward through Anhwei
province. Although there was initial success, the two generals bick-
ered continuously, and in the fifth month of 1163, the Chin Tartars
took advantage of the confusion to deliver the Chinese armies a
crushing defeat at Fu-li in modern Kiangsu province. Chang Chün
was immediately demoted and the counterattack ground to a halt.

Yang heard of all these tragic events while on the road to the
capital city and quickly realized that his hopes of high position were
now completely dashed. However, he continued on his journey and
eventually reached the capital Hangchow at the end of the year.
Although Chang Chün had been demoted, he still held an official
position in the central government, and he attempted to recom-
mend Yang to the authorities. At the time Yang visited Hangchow it
was the largest city in the world, with a population in excess of one
million. Yang did not like big cities, and he did not write any poems
about the dazzling New Year festivities which he certainly witnessed. However, he did join his new friends in a number of excursions
to certain famous beauty spots around the capital, which were practically obligatory for a young poet to visit. While visiting West Lake
he wrote:

> Misty boats, horizontal, sideways, lie in willow port bays;
> Cloudy mountains appear and disappear midst willow rows.
> How could mountain climbing equal wandering by this lake?
> For on the water's surface, I can see all the mountains I want![8]

Due to the good offices of Chang Chün, Yang was offered a minor
post in the central government sometime in the first month of 1164,
but Yang was not fated for higher official service, for shortly before

the first full moon of the New Year, he received news that his father was very ill, and he quickly set out on the path home. By the time Yang arrived, his father was already dead, and Yang commenced the three year's mourning period at home. After a few months, he was further grieved to hear that his mentor Chang Chün had also passed away after he had left the capital. He obviously realized that his future hopes for an official career were considerably dimmed, but, in any case, he could take no new post until the three year period was finished.

When Yang Wan-li returned to Hangchow sometime close to New Year of 1167, he discovered that the political situation had changed completely from the heyday of Chang Chün. The general's fall from favor had not precipitated a violent purge of the pro-war faction, but their warnings concerning the Chin peril went unheeded by the emperor Hsiao-tsung, and virtual peace reigned between the two governments for the next forty-odd years. All the same, ardent patriots sent up countless memorials to the emperor urging attack, but Yang learned the result of these labors after talking to a minor official he befriended in the capital:

A Colophon on the Memorial of Ten Thousand Words by the *Fu-kan* Wei Chih-yao from Szechwan

Short lamp midst the rain, his hair is like snow;[9]
A traveler with long sword, he is given no fish to eat.[10]
Why take the trouble of sending up memorials with such mournful cries?
For truly the men of *this* age respect only Master Fiction![11]

Yang quickly realized that he could not obtain a central government post under the conditions existing in the capital, yet he remained there until the autumn of the year, discussing the political situation with friends. It also seems that his disenchantment with the government caused him to take an increasing interest in Ch'an (Zen) Buddhism, for references to the religion become steadily commoner in his poetry of this period. In one poem to a friend Yang alludes to "Questions and answers in the monk's room, the lion roars."[12] This is a specific reference to the method of teaching used by the Lin-chi Sect of Ch'an Buddhists, in which the monk answers his students' questions with a bewildering statement to destroy their tendency to rational thought. Lin-chi masters also frequently shouted, that is, "roared," at their students and even pummeled them with a club at times. When Yang finally returned to his home in Chi-shui he had reached the depth of his depression, and he began to feel that both officialdom and Buddhist enlightenment were beyond his reach: "Select officialdom or Buddhism; *both* remote, remote; / They never concerned me from the beginning, so I become recklessly depressed."[13]

Yang remained in Chi-shui for the next two years of his life, meeting friends, writing poetry, and waiting for an opportunity. He had already reached the age of forty without any outstanding accomplishments in either literature or politics, so when his eyes began to fail, he became distraught:

> Because of my Aging Eyes I Sigh as I Give up Books
>
> I'm old, and books no longer have any place;
> After all, my eyes are already fuzzy.
> Ink soldiers are not friends to one's death;
> Cassia wine seems to be *my* livelihood.
> After snow, the frost becomes sharper;
> While chanting poetry, my hat lies crooked.
> My small son knows I'm just lazy;
> Reciting lessons at night, he raises a racket on purpose![14]

IV   *Recalled to Office*

At long last Yang's talents were recognized, for in the beginning of 1170, he was appointed governor of Feng-hsin County, which was not much over a hundred miles to the north of Chi-shui. According to Yang's biographers, he was a model governor, who adopted a *laissez-faire* policy toward the people in his district. When people owed tax money to the government, Yang did not send collectors into the countryside to force collection but merely displayed the names of offenders in the market place. We are assured that every one promptly paid his back taxes! However, Yang did not enjoy his new work very much, for he found it so time-consuming as to interfere with his writing. In the middle of busy travels about the district he wrote:

> Passing West Mountain
>
> In one year I've trodden the road past West Mountain twice;
> West Mountain laughs at me, for he knows enough to say:

"Your breast is brimming with a hundred gallons of
    red and black ink dust,[15]
But you don't even have half a line like 'winding
    the pearl curtain in the rain.' "[16]
Out of politeness I buy wine and thank West Mountain:
"I'm grateful for your mountain scenery; you've given
    me a lift.
Yet my temple hairs are turning white from collecting taxes,
And even if dust filled my whole breast, when would
    I have time to worry about it?"[17]

Yang had no desire to continue in one local post after another, and
his ambitions were clearly set on the capital city. In order to gain
attention, he busied himself with preparing a large treatise on
government in thirty chapters, which he entitled "A Policy of a
Thousand Precautions." Yang's efforts were not buried in the mass
of paperwork at the capital, and the prime minister was quite impressed. Therefore, in the tenth month of 1170, he was given the
post of Professor of the Directorate of Education *(Kuo-tzu Po-shih)*
and Yang set out for Hangchow immediately.

Yang's treatise was not marked by any striking novelty, but
neither was his work calculated to make friends with all persons in
high, influential positions. In a chapter entitled "Government of the
People" Yang wrote:

I have heard that the people are the life of the state but the enemy of the
officials. The officials are the delight of the prince but the distress of the
state. The rise and fall of empires and the length of dynasties are all dependent on this principle. Yet, what evil do the officials do against the people
that the people hate them? The officials are not really enemies of the
people. Yet if they do not treat the people as enemies the high officials will
be without merit, and their subordinates will have fault. Fear of fault drives
the officials from behind while merit entices them from ahead. Although
they do not wish to be enemies of the people, there is no way out for
them.[18]

After this general discussion Yang proceeded to apply his ideas to
recent events in the Sung empire:

On the streets I have heard that the rising of the Lin Bandits last year was
brought on by local officials who administered the "equal grain purchase"
poorly.[19] Did anyone tell His Majesty of this? The whole empire knew that

the court was intending to eliminate all such taxes. Nevertheless, I have also heard that among certain commanderies of Kiangsi, a Commandery X, which does not produce silk, said to the court that it desired to buy silk from Commandery Y. What does this mean? There is nothing the people despise more than doing business with the officials. It starts out as "business" but ends up being confiscation. That is why a Sage is careful about beginnings. Now, the various cities in Commandery Y are additionally being levied for silk in an amount equal to their normal taxes, but the people are not being reimbursed with money for this extra amount. People who do not acquiesce are punished by the officials. Supposedly they are being punished for not paying their normal taxes, but in reality these cruel exactions are being made for the neighboring Commandery X. Moreover, the so-called "equal buying"[20] is already included in their standard taxes, along with the so-called "Huai uniforms tax."[21] Now we also demand silk from them for the neighboring commandery. These three types of tax along with the silk of the standard taxes are a four-fold exaction. How can the people stand this? Yet the officials do not let you know.[22]

Yang's policies were hardly of the sort to win him friends in the court or among the more corrupt local officials, so when he arrived in Hangchow shortly after New Year's day in 1171, he immediately became involved in the swirl of the capital's politics. In that year the emperor Hsiao-tsung attempted to appoint his son-in-law to an influential position in the military. Many officials felt the man was totally incompetent and a public uproar ensued. The opposition to the emperor was centered around Chang Shih, the son of Yang Wan-li's mentor, Chang Chün. Chang Shih violently attacked the new appointment in open court, for he felt that the emperor's son-in-law could only add to the military confusion of the Southern Sung dynasty. When Chang Shih was demoted to a local government post, Yang Wan-li came to his defense, and Yang's biographers tell us that his bravery inspired so much admiration in the court that the emperor decided to leave him alone rather than stir up more public disapproval.

Yang spent two more rather uneventful years in the court, but in 1174 he was given a position as governor of Chang-chou in Fukien province. However, he was not pleased with the new post offered him and returned to Chi-shui instead. Yang was becoming increasingly disillusioned with official life, and it is possible that he was eager for a rest from the grind of public service. During the two years he spent in retirement, Yang wrote poetry and engaged in gardening projects. He was particularly delighted by a small library pavilion called the Snow Angling Boat, which he had constructed the first year he was back in Chi-shui:

I Sleep Exhausted at Snow Angling Boat[23]

I made a small study, which was shaped like a boat, so I named it Snow Angling Boat. While reading there, I fell asleep from exhaustion. Suddenly a breeze entered the door and stirred up an overwhelming fragrance from some plum flowers in a vase. I was startled awake and wrote the following short poem.

Small pavilion, bright window, I close the door half way;
Reading books, I fall asleep——zzzzzz, zzzzzz.
For no reason at all, I'm disturbed by these plum flowers,
Who blow their perfume at me on purpose and smash
    my sweet dreams.[24]

This period of leisure also allowed Yang to continue his studies of Ch'an Buddhism, which had occupied second place only to his poetic writing. When he mailed a poem to an old friend who was serving in Kuangtung, Yang wrote: "Since my friend left me it's been exactly three years/ With whom can I discuss poetry and expound on Ch'an?"[25] Yang Wan-li had already started to reject the bookishness of the scholar tradition, an attitude which harmonized with Ch'an tenets:

Reading Books

Reading books, I don't tire of the toil,
But working too hard makes me fatigued and dizzy.
I'd best sit meditating with my books;
So the books and I can *both* forget words.[26]
When I feel like it, I open the pages,
And suddenly arrive at the Source of the Hundred Sages.
I say I'm enlightened, but there never was any enlightenment;
I speak of mystery, but from the beginning there's
    been no mystery.[27]
When I find something that suits my mind,
All I feel is total rapture.
Who is it that makes this pleasure?
Neither I nor Heaven.
I laugh at myself; I've never been right;
I throw down my book at the foot of the pillow![28]

V *Sudden Enlightenment*

Yang's period of idleness soon came to an end, for in the fourth month of 1178, he set out from Chi-shui to become governor of Ch'ang-chou in Kiangsi province. After arriving at his new post he became so busy with paperwork and other trifling duties that he had practically no time for poetry. In fact, Yang was a man caught in a spiritual and literary crisis when he arrived in Ch'ang-chou. He certainly realized that high position was never to be his, and so his only claim to fame was his poetry. Yang had already reached the age of fifty by now, and although he had written much fine poetry, he still did not qualify as a great poet. And yet, the T'ang master Tu Fu (712–770) had died when he was only fifty-eight.

Nevertheless, spiritual crises frequently lead to sudden "conversions," and Yang was no exception in this respect, for at the beginning of 1178, he had an experience, which in its depth and suddenness, was very similar to the profound sudden enlightenment of the Ch'an monk: "On New Year's Day of 1178, I started to write poetry, because I was on vacation and had no official business. Suddenly, I was as if enlightened *(wu)*. . . . I was so overjoyed, I tried having my son hold the writing brush while I orally composed several poems, and they came gushing forth without any of the earlier grinding."[29]

Yang Wan-li had experienced a profound awakening of his poetic creativity, for in the single year of 1178 he wrote more poems than he had in the previous eight years, and this great burst of writing came while he was busily engaged with local government. In a poem written soon after his enlightenment, Yang describes the new ease which he felt in writing:

Drinking Late

> One by one I recite the poems, one by one, copy them;
> I have a cup of wild vegetables and mountain dainties, too.
> The spring almost doesn't brace up my drunkeness
> When the moon arrives at the tiptop branch of the plums.[30]

Yang Wan-li's poetic enlightenment had been preceded by a much greater awareness of Ch'an, as we have already seen. Although it would be hazardous to guess Yang's spiritual level in 1178, it seems that his poetic enlightenment was only part of a wider spiritual enlightenment. Though he does not inform us of any sudden awakening in the purely Buddhist sense, a poem he wrote in the same year describes a mystical experience of the Buddhist variety:

While on Vacation, I Read Books at Abundant Planting Pavilion on a Clear Morning

Since I brought my family to Ching-ch'i,
A year has suddenly passed.
My official residence isn't really bad,
But my feelings are always joyless.
If my servants don't get sick,
Then my children are crying for sure.
Formerly I was poor, sighing because of hunger;
But this autumn it's not hunger that bothers me.
In morning I get up with a book in my sleeve,
And quickly climb to the pavilion to enjoy myself.
Traces of dew, stars and moon still remain;
Winds and air, no windows or shutters.
Suddenly I feel my old sick body
Can't stand these robes of linen any more.
How did I make it through yesterday's heat?
The morning coolness is what I treasure!
White birds far off look like butterflies;
Black locusts hum like poets chanting.
Pine trees' color turns my spirit to snow;
Fragrance of lotuses ices my gall.
Suddenly, where have happiness and sorrow gone?
My body, too, disappears completely.
My children don't understand anything at all,
For they call me to come home and eat breakfast.[31]

The "old, sick body" of which Yang speaks is the body that the Buddhists say suffers from old age, sickness, and death. In a flash of intuition, Yang leaves this body and transcends the duality between happiness and sorrow.

Yang's children calling him from his state of enlightenment to attend to more practical matters such as eating breakfast suggests that his spiritual quests were limited by mundane considerations. However, for the Ch'an Buddhist, true enlightenment consists in the realization that illusion and reality are identical and that the life of the ordinary world is the same as the life of the enlightened. The

ideal of the Ch'an school and, indeed, of most other Chinese schools
of Buddhist thought was the legendary figure Vimalakīrti, a rich
merchant who lived fully in the world of action and yet possessed a
richer understanding of the Buddhist doctrine than the monk disciples of Buddha, who engaged in constant meditation and fasting.[32]
It was at about this period in Yang's life that he realized the truth of
this Vimalakīrti ideal:

Approaching Holidays

During the holidays I'm not without work,
Busy, I am by nature at leisure.
I ask the wind to trouble a white bird
And send a letter inviting the green mountain.
A collection of poetry, one or two volumes;
My library, three or four rooms.
When I feel like it, I can write poetry,
Yet I *still* insist on saying I'm in the world of dust![33]

In Yang's condition his leisure is his business and his business, his
leisure, and he is both within and outside of the world of dust.

VI *Later Career*

Yang's fertile period in Ch'ang-chou came to an end in 1179,
when the central government sent word that he had been appointed
to a new local position in Kuangtung province. He first returned
home for a visit with his family, and after the New Year's celebrations of 1180, Yang set forth on the long and perilous journey south
to Canton. After arriving at his new post, he rapidly became
acclimatized to his new environment and proceeded to explore the
natural phenomena of tropical China. One of the most delightful
products of Kuangtung is the lichee, and judging by the number of
poems Yang wrote about this fruit, he considered eating it one of the
high points of his visit:

On the Eighth of the Fourth Month I Eat New Lichees

A little spot of rouge dyes it stems' edges,
Then suddenly red covers its green robe entirely.[34]
Its purple jade bones are as slender as the clove,
While its snow white flesh is cool even in the noon heat.

How can I touch this icy pellet lying on my palm?[35]
Still its flavor with wine is hard to forget!
This old glutton wants to eat three hundred lichees,
But I fear their sweet chill will freeze my intestines
   to pieces![36]

Yang's peaceful career as a provincial official was soon disturbed, for in 1181 Kuangtung was invaded by a bandit army, and Yang Wan-li was commanded by the central government to suppress the uprising. Yang accepted his new responsibility with considerable trepidation, and one wonders how he felt engaging in the slaughter of lower class bandits, who most likely revolted because of the excessive taxation he had criticized in his earlier writings. Nonetheless, he was totally successful in the enterprise, and his victory was of immediate advantage to his political career.

When the emperor heard of his exploits, Yang was quickly recalled for service in the central government, and at the end of 1181, he headed back to the capital Hangchow. He never reached the capital, however, because his mother died in 1182, and he now had to wait out the expected three year mourning period. Yang's observation of his mother's mourning was much stricter than after his father's earlier death. Not only did Yang refuse the official post offered him as would be customary, but he also stopped all literary activity for the next three years. He was now a famous man, and society expected him to display a greater degree of filial piety than during his more obscure youth.

In 1184 Yang's mourning came to an end, and in the eleventh month, he was appointed Assistant Officer of the Ministry of Personnel *(li-pu yüan-wai-lang)*. During the next three years Yang gradually rose in the bureaucracy, but by the end of 1187, he was once more in trouble with the authorities. The retired emperor Kao-tsung had died in the tenth month of that year, and his son Hsiao-tsung (reg. 1163–1190) turned over the reins of the government to the incompetent crown prince, the future emperor Kuang-tsung (reg. 1190–1195), so that Hsiao-tsung could observe the three year mourning period. Yang felt that the government was confused enough already, so he sent a strong protest to Hsiao-tsung and attempted to resign from his post but was refused permission. In 1188 Yang Wan-li became further embroiled in court strife, because when a high government official petitioned the emperor to make

sacrifice to dead military and political figures of the deceased emperor Kao-tsung's reign, the name of Yang Wan-li's mentor, Chang
Chün, was omitted from the list. This action was an intended insult
against the war party to which Yang belonged, and during the ensu-
ing uproar Yang managed not only to alienate the high official who
initiated the sacrifice but also to insult the emperor Hsiao-tsung by
comparing him to the universally detested first emperor of China,
Ch'in Shih-huang (reg. 221–209 B.C.). In the fourth month of 1188
Yang Wan-li was demoted to the post of governor of Yün-chou in
southern Kiangsi province.

However, when Yang Wan-li left the capital, he seemed to be
deeply relieved, because now he was free from the pressures of the
constant political struggles in Hangchow. His trip to Yün-chou was
extremely leisurely, and when he finally arrived there, he spent
much of his time traveling about and enjoying the local sights. He
renewed his interests in Ch'an Buddhism and frequently compared
himself to a Buddhist monk during this period. When sending off a
friend to the capital, Yang wrote:

Sending off Tseng Wu-yi to Become a Historian

Jade rainbows race in the water of Lucky Pattern River;
My home was to the west of the water, yours to the east.
Whenever we thought of each other, we ordered carriages,
And on adjoining couches, listened to pine wind in
    the night's rain.
Meanwhile, poor officials, we scattered our separate ways;
I was a south flying honker, you, a north flying goose.
This morning the post rider knocks on the watch tower gate:
"A guest! A guest has come to see you!"
I hear you are taking your family to the emperor's capital;
Beating drums, you set off by boat, traveling up to "heaven."
Still, you were kind enough to go out of your way a few miles
To come and visit this monk in his hermitage at Kiangsi.
Two poet immortals reside in the Imperial Secretariat[37]
Midst red peonies, green moss, and purple myrtle shadows.
If they ask you what this mountain monk is doing:
As the day grows late and orioles sing, he sleeps and never
    wakes up![38]

Yang Wan-li hoped that the world would leave him alone for the
rest of his life, but political events altered his plans for retirement.

In the second month of 1189, Hsiao-tsung formally abdicated his throne in favor of the crown prince, who now became the new emperor Kuang-tsung. Six months later Yang Wan-li was called back to the capital as Director of the Imperial Library *(mi-shu chien)*, and he arrived in Hangchow during the ninth month. Kuang-tsung was completely useless, and his empress attempted to gain power by sowing dissension between the emperor and his retired father.

Luckily for Yang Wan-li, he did not need to become caught up in the internal dissension of the court, because in the twelfth month, he was appointed Welcoming and Accompanying Ambassador *(chieh-pan shih)* to the Chin Tartars, and, thus, he was able to leave the capital on a lengthy voyage to the boundary between the two states, where he was to receive the Chin ambassador sent to congratulate the Sung emperor on the New Year. Yang's trip northward from Hangchow started out auspiciously, and as he crossed the Yangtze River he wrote:

Crossing the Yangtze River
(Second Poem of Two)

Heaven made this natural moat to protect skies of our
    southern Wu;[39]
It's equal to Yao-han, a pass where two can hold off
    a hundred.[40]
This ten thousand mile silver river drains into the
    jasper sea,
And a pair of jade pagodas outline Metal Mountain.
Banners and flags on the other shore, Huai-nan is close;
Drums and trumpets blare midst frost; all calm north
    of the frontier.
Many thanks to the River God, for the wind is just right;
I cross a thousand acres of vast waves in an instant.[41]

On the surface, the poem is a celebration of a pleasant journey across the river, but Yang was obviously aware that a river he could so easily cross could also be navigated by Chin warships. However, as Yang approached the boundary with the Chin Tartars, his indignation grew:

The generals Liu Ch'i, Yüeh Fei, Chang Chün, and
    Han Shih-chung proclaimed our country's might;

While the prime ministers Chao Tung and Chang Chün
built the imperial foundation.[42]
Within a foot, the long Huai River divides us into North
and South;
My tears moisten the autumn wind—who is to blame for this?[43]

Yang Wan-li was not an effusive poet, and it is very rare that the
word "tears" is even mentioned in his verse, in contrast to many
T'ang and earlier poets. Yang's tears were tears of rage over the
unforgivable political and military blunders of the Southern Sung.
Three of the generals mentioned, Liu Ch'i (d. 1158), Yüeh Fei, and
Han Shih-chung, were all eliminated by the first Southern Sung
emperor's cruel prime minister Ch'in Kuei, and we have already
seen the treatment meted out to Yang Wan-li's mentor, the general
Chang Chün. Yang clearly knew whom he could blame for the
disaster that had lost half of China to the Chin Tartars.

Yang returned to the capital about New Year of 1190 and was
given an assignment as Reviser of the Veritable Records (shih-lu
chien-t'ao), in which he was supposed to help in the preparation of
the historical records for the long twenty-seven year reign of the
now retired emperor Hsiao-tsung. In the eleventh month the so-
called Sagely Government of Hsiao-tsung was completed by the
court historians, and Yang Wan-li was appointed to be one of the
scholars who would present the book to the retired emperor. When
Hsiao-tsung saw Yang's name on the list, he became extremely
vexed and is reported to have asked his son Kuang-tsung: "What is
Yang Wan-li still doing here?"[44] Kuang-tsung at first feigned ignorance, but his father was so furious that not only was Yang prevented
from taking part in the presentation ceremonies but he was also
immediately demoted to the local post of Assistant Fiscal Intendant
for Chiang-tung (Chiang-tung chuan-yün shih).

Unperturbed by all these events, Yang headed for Nanking.
However, he was not even fated to remain there for long, because
he soon clashed with the central government over new plans to issue
a virtually worthless paper currency in the area under his jurisdic-
tion. The currency was theoretically based on iron coinage, but it
just so happened that the government itself prohibited the circula-
tion of iron coins in Yang's area. Yang refused to carry out government orders, offending the prime minister. When in the eighth
month of 1192, he was transferred to a new post, Yang sent in his

resignation, which was accepted. Yang arrived back in his native village Chi-shui before the beginning of autumn, and since he was already sixty-five, he had no further intention of serving the government. Shortly after his retirement, Yang wrote:

Watering a Pot of Calamus and Narcissus Flowers

When I reread old poems, they become new again;
After finishing them, I'm so drowsy I stretch and yawn.
Innumerable flowers in the pot complain of their thirst,
But this old fellow only wants to be a lazy man![45]

VII *Retirement*

During the rest of his life, Yang lived at Chi-shui in virtual isolation, taking occasional excursions around the nearby countryside and still busily writing poetry. The poetry of these last fourteen years was gathered posthumously by Yang's eldest son, but all of the poet's earlier works had already been printed by this time. Yang was fully aware that he was one of the major literary figures of his period, and although he suffered from increasingly bad health in his seventies, his poetic output hardly diminished. When he was seventy-eight years of age, Yang wrote:

After a relapse of bladder disease the doctor told me to avoid writing because it strains my heart, so when I got up in the morning I warned myself with the following poem.

(Second Poem of Two)

Recklessly addicted to poetry, I tire my heart in vain;
So I beg forgiveness from orioles, flowers for stopping my bitter chant.
I don't owe any debts to T'ao Ch'ien or Hsieh Ling-yün;[46]
So why do *they* come looking for me at night in my dreams?[47]

By this time it seems that the old poet had totally transcended the concerns of the everyday world and was living in a state of nearly perfect detachment.

The reason for Yang Wan-li's peace of mind is that he had reaffirmed the Vimalakīrti ideal which he had discovered in middle age. References to the Indian sage become commoner in his later poetry, and the philosophy of living both within and without the world of dust is expressed in a number of Yang Wan-li's late poems:

The Realm of Idleness

If you want to hold fast to the Realm of Idleness,
It's not outside the Mundane Realm.
Bright moon and pure wind,
When don't we face each other?[48]

Such an approach to life allowed Yang to bear the most excruciating
pain with good humor:

While ill, my feet start hurting again. After I sit exhausted the whole day, I
write the following to be rid of my depression.

Flowers fill my eyes, and snow covers my head;
I have passed three or four years in uncertainty.
Who would know my ailing legs keep me from walking?
If people saw me crouching, they'd say I was meditating!
I drop my fan by the table side, but I'm too lazy to pick it up,
So how can I possibly hunt for my book beneath the window?
Men of the world are always envious of flying immortals,
But men who can walk seem like immortals to *me*![49]

Yang's illness obviously reminded him of the famous malady of
Vimalakīrti, for when some relatives and friends came to visit him
he wrote: "Vimalakīrti's grave illness was not easy to cure,/But as
soon as Mañjuśri asked the question, he lost his baleful malady.[50]
The *Vimalakīrti-nirdeśa-sūtra*, or the *Sūtra on the Teachings of
Vimalakīrti*, starts with the Buddha attempting to send one of his
disciples to visit Vimalakīrti, who has recently fallen ill. However,
when all of Buddha's disciples refuse to go out of fear that the sage
will expose their inferior knowledge of Buddhist philosophy, the
bodhisattva of knowledge, Mañjuśrī, agrees to lead them. This
meeting of the Buddha, Mañjuśri, and the numerous disciples at
Vimalakīrti's mansion becomes the occasion for a profound discussion of Buddhism, which culminates in Mañjuśri asking each of the
bodhisattvas to give his explanation of the Buddhist doctrine. Each
provides a complex answer, but when it is Vimalakīrti's turn to
speak, he remains silent. This is the "thunderous silence" of Vimalakīrti so often referred to by Ch'an and other Chinese Buddhists,
and it is this same realization of Vimalakīrti's truth which enabled
Yang to transcend the worries and illnesses of his later years.[51]

Despite Yang's retirement from public service, there was much to worry about, for the court had been in turmoil ever since Yang had left it. When the retired emperor Hsiao-tsung died, his son Kuang-tsung, who had developed an uncontrollable hatred for his father, refused to take part in any of the funeral ceremonies. A powerful official by the name of Han T'o-chou (d. 1207) used this occasion to conspire against Kuang-tsung and in 1195 had him removed from the throne in favor of the next emperor, Ning-tsung (reg. 1195–1225). Han T'o-chou's power grew rapidly, and when he began to encounter opposition from a majority of scholar-officials at the court, he moved quickly to purge his enemies from the central government. In 1195 Han had attempted to recall Yang Wan-li back to public service, but Yang intelligently refused, giving bad health as an excuse. Yang incurred Han T'o-chou's everlasting hatred when the poet refused to write an essay celebrating the opening of a garden Han had constructed by the lavish use of public funds.

Han T'o-chou had finally eliminated all of his enemies at court, but since he was not able to gain acceptance from the intellectuals, he felt that the only way to consolidate his position was to engage in military adventures. There had been peace between the Chin and the Sung for over thirty years, but when a Chinese ambassador returned from the Chin court, he reported that the enemy's government was in complete disarray and the country ripe for invasion. By 1204 Han T'o-chou had started massive preparations for an invasion of the north. In 1205 Han summoned Yang back to the capital once again, but instead of merely politely refusing on grounds of health, Yang sent a reply accusing Han T'o-chou of undermining the security of the state. Yang's memorial was suppressed by Han's friends, but it probably would not have affected imperial policy anyway, for in 1206 Han T'o-chou unleashed his attack against the Chin Tartars. Although there were some initial successes, the Chin had long ago gotten wind of Chinese intentions, and they were so well prepared that they were soon turning the Sung offensive into a general rout. The Chinese army collapsed when Han's most trusted general deserted to the enemy.

All of these disastrous setbacks had been hidden from Yang Wan-li by his family, but one day in the fifth month of 1206, a distant relative who had recently returned from the capital informed Yang of all that had transpired. Yang's official biography says that the poet "cried so mournfully he lost his voice. He repeatedly called for paper and wrote: 'Han T'o-chou is a traitorous minister. He has monopolized power as if without a superior, mobilized the army to harm the people, and plans to endanger the nation's ancestral altars. Although I still have my head, there is no way for me to avenge the state. I can only indulge in lone indignation.' Then after he had written fourteen words as a parting message to his wife and children, his writing brush fell, and he passed away."[52] Although this account was probably manufactured by Yang's biographers for dramatic effect, anger at Han T'o-chou's campaign could easily have hastened Yang Wan-li's demise. Yang had always been in favor of a military reconquest of North China, but he was acutely aware of the poor state of Sung military preparation and the self-seeking nature of Han T'o-chou's plans for attacking the Chin. In any event, Yang's opinion of Han was born out by subsequent events, for in 1207 the minister was assassinated with the connivance of the emperor, and in 1208 his head was sent in a special case to the Chin court.

Yang Wan-li was buried in his native village of Chi-shui where his tomb can still be seen today. In 1208 his eldest son gathered together the poetry Yang had written after his retirement, and some years later the earlier collections and this last collection were published together with Yang Wan-li's prose writings under the title *Ch'eng-chai chi*, or *The Collected Works of Sincere Studio*. Altogether there are about three thousand two hundred poems in this collection, and Yang's complete prose writings comprise about eight hundred and twenty pages in the modern *Ssu-pu ts'ung-k'an* edition.

Although Yang Wan-li had pursued a public career, which was expected of any educated man in Sung China, he seems to have controlled all ambitions he had for high office with a very strong sense of moral propriety. When he retired from his position in Nanking, he was entitled to ten thousand strings of cash but left the money in the public treasury instead. His home in Chi-shui was extremely simple, and the Yang family did not enlarge or decorate it during three generations.[53] Describing a man as an outspoken critic of corrupt government is a favorite Confucian cliché, but Yang's frankness frequently harmed his advancement in office. In short, Yang Wan-li came close to living up to the Confucian ideal of public service.

But as we have seen, Confucianism was by no means the only philosophy that guided Yang's life, and he must have reached near perfection in his realization of the Ch'an ideal, too. A few years before he died, Yang wrote:

> It doesn't matter whether one stays home or goes out,
> For you transcend the world while in its midst.[54]

CHAPTER 2

Theory of Literature

I Ch'an and Early Sung Poetry

IN our study of Yang Wan-li's political career and private life, we have already touched upon the extreme importance of Ch'an Buddhism to his spiritual and literary development. In the following discussion of Yang's theory of literature, we shall see that Ch'an Buddhism played an equally important role in forming his views on the writing of poetry. Although Buddhism was certainly one of the major philosophical schools which inspired earlier Chinese poets, one encounters much difficulty in defining the relationship between Buddhism and poetry in Chinese verse, because Chinese poets rarely limited themselves to the study of any one particular philosophy. The greatest confusion arises when we deal with what appears to be pure nature poetry, and very frequently is. It is very easy for the literary critic with a background in Buddhist thought to regard such images as falling plum flowers as symbolic of worldly impermanence, but he may be reading something into the poem which the poet never intended. Earlier Chinese poets rarely help us in solving our dilemma, and only in Sung times, when poets started composing "poetry talks" and literary critical poems in a fairly large quantity, can we obtain a very clear picture of the poetical views that the principal Chinese poets held.

Although the founders of the various Ch'an Buddhist sects had lived in the T'ang dynasty, the literary output of Ch'an Buddhism reached its high point in Sung times. One of our most important sources of Ch'an history, *The Record of the Transmission of the Lamp of the Ching-te Era (Ching-te ch'uan-teng lu)* was compiled about 1004, whereas the two most widely used *kung-an* (Japanese *kō-an*) collections, *The Records of the Green Cliff (Pi-yen lu)* and the *Pass Without a Gate (Wu-men kuan)*, were written in 1125 and

38

1228, respectively. Even the collected sayings of the T'ang masters were frequently reedited by Sung writers and quite often did not receive their final form until Sung times. Most important of all, in Sung times Ch'an Buddhism penetrated deeply into the intellectual and cultural life of the Chinese educated classes, and, thus, served as a stimulus to many of the finest elements of Chinese culture.

Su Shih (1037–1101), the foremost poet of the Northern Sung period, was strongly influenced by Buddhist ideas. In a poem presented to a Ch'an master he was sending off, Su wrote of the intimate connection between the Buddhist mystical experience and the creation of poetry:

> If you want your poetry to be miraculous,
> Don't despise emptiness and tranquility.
> Tranquil, you comprehend the multitude of movements;
> Empty, you take in the myriad realms.
> Experiencing the world, you walk amidst men;
> Contemplating your body, you lie on a cloudy ridge.
> As to salty and sour, there are a host of preferences;
> But in their midst lies a great flavor, everlasting.
> Poetry and the Buddhist *dharma* don't hinder one another,
> So I should ask you more about these ideas.[1]

Su Shih's emphasis on emptiness and tranquility and his notion that an ultimate unity ("flavor") lies behind the phenomena of the world are definitely of Buddhist inspiration but not specifically Ch'an. However, when he says, "Good poems burst out of my mouth, who can choose them?" one suspects that his theory of poetry has been influenced by the Ch'an concept of spontaneity in the enlightened person.[2]

Nevertheless, it was not until the generation of poets following Su Shih that the Ch'an Buddhist experience was closely linked to the poetic creative process. Su Shih had displayed signs of Ch'an influence, but one of his students, Han Chü (d. 1135), seems to have been one of the earliest poets who clearly stated that the process of studying poetry was the same as Ch'an meditation:

> Studying poetry, you should be like one starting to study Ch'an;
> Before you are enlightened, you must meditate on various methods.
> One day, when you are enlightened to the true *dharma* eye,
> Your hand will draw forth the poetry by itself, stanzas ready-made.[3]

Furthermore, he is supposed to have said: "The Way of poetry is
like the Buddha *dharma*, for it must be separated into great and
small vehicles [that is Hīnayāna and Mahāyāna] and a heterodox,
demon, external path. Only the knowing can speak of this."[4] Han
Chü's equation of poetic creativity to Ch'an meditation is much
clearer than anything found in Su Shih's writings, and yet Han's
emphasis on spontaneity in the process of writing poetry is clearly
connected to Su's earlier statements on this matter. It is interesting
to note that Su Shih himself considered Han Chü to be close in style
to the T'ang poet Ch'u Kuang-hsi (fl. 742), a Buddhist nature poet.
After Su Shih's time, the critic Lü Pen-chung (ca. 1119) included
Han Chü in the Kiangsi School of poetry, but Han himself finally
disagreed with Lü's classification, and the Ch'an element in Han's
theory of poetry seems to justify his view that he differed from the
Kiangsi authors.[5]

Another Northern Sung poet Wu K'o (ca. 1126) saw the poet's
process of creation as similar to Ch'an enlightenment:

Studying poetry is entirely like studying Ch'an;
Bamboo bed, meditation cushion, you can't count the years.
Finally when you comprehend everything yourself,
You can easily draw it forth and are transcendent.[6]

Once again we see the concept that the creation of poetry is a
natural act which becomes almost effortless after one has attained
enlightenment.

II *Yang Wan-li and Ch'an*

Yang Wan-li's own development as a poet bears a marked resemblance to the spiritual progress of the great Ch'an masters of the
T'ang and Sung periods. Although their final enlightenment is usually described as sudden, it was frequently preceded by rigorous
discipline and lengthy study under a number of masters. For Yang,
the path to the final enlightenment, which enabled him to rise
above the mediocrity of his youthful verse and create a new style,
was as painful as the Ch'an student's subjection to the master's
bewildering paradoxes and irrational beatings:

I first imitated the poetry of the gentlemen from Kiangsi, following which I
studied the five-character regulated verse of Ch'en Shih-tao [1053–1101].
Then I studied the seven-character short poems of Wang An-shih [1021–

1086], and, finally, the short poems of the T'ang poets. But the more I studied, the less I was able to write. Once I complained about this to Lin Kuang-ch'ao [1114–1178], who replied, "When you are so choosy, it is hard to get what you want, so how could you hope for your works to be many?" I sighed and said, "Poets have different defects which yet arise from the same source, and I am surely not alone in this!" Thus, from the spring of 1177 all the way back to 1162, I had written only five hundred eighty-two poems; so few they were! In the summer I went to my official position in Ching-ch'i, and as soon as I assumed my post, I read lawsuits and arranged the local revenue, up to my head in paperwork. Ideas for poems raced back and forth in my mind from time to time, but although I wanted to write, I didn't have any leisure. On New Year's Day of 1178, I started to write poetry, because I was on vacation and had no official business. Suddenly, I was as if enlightened (*wu*), and at that moment I took leave of the T'ang poets, of Wang An-shih and Ch'en Shih-tao, and of all the gentlemen of Kiangsi, no longer daring to imitate any of them. I was so overjoyed, I tried having my son hold the writing brush while I orally composed several poems, and they came gushing forth without any of the earlier grinding.[7]

Again and again, we read of similar experiences in the Ch'an literature. The monk Ling-yu (771–853), one of the founders of the Kuei-yang Sect, left his family at the age of fifteen and spent eight years "studying the sūtras and discipline of the great and small vehicles" before he was brought to sudden enlightenment by his master Pai-chang (720–814).[8] Similarly, Wen-yen (864–949), founder of the Yün-men Sect, made an exhaustive study of Buddhist discipline under his first teacher before he obtained sudden enlightenment under his later master Mu-chou (*ca.* 875).[9]

In two poems written in 1166, over ten years before his poetical enlightenment, Yang touches on a number of the ideas that later became important in his poetry. Although these poems have little literary value, since they were written in Yang's early imitative style, they can serve as a framework within which we can discuss the basic concepts of Yang's theory of poetry:

In Answer to Li T'ien-lin

I

In studying poetry, one must be penetrating and free;
Then, trusting his hand, one is lone and exalted.
The robe and the begging bowl are timeless,
And a hill or mountain is just one hair.

In your own lines—"the pool has grass;"[10]
Beyond words, your eyes all in disorder.[11]
What then does the delicious resemble?
Frosty crab with some wine dregs.

II

The *dharma* of poetry is hard for heaven to keep secret;
All you do is add your own labor.
When in meditation—a cedar tree;[12]
Finally enlightened, how still a peach flower?[13]
I want to share an east or west jade wine cup,
But we are as far apart as the north and south shores.
Are you willing to come and talk this over with me?
We will sit aside on a white seagull sandbank.[14]

Although these two poems are even more uncomfortable to read in the Chinese original than in English translation, they are very important for an understanding of Yang Wan-li's literary theory. In the first two lines of our first poem, Yang is saying that once the poet is enlightened, that is, "penetrating and free," he obtains his own independent style in a totally spontaneous manner, for he can now trust his hand to compose poetry without any conscious effort. We have already noted that Yang found writing more natural after he had been enlightened and was no longer dependent on his old masters. Now the writing of poetry is a natural act that the poet himself cannot control:

From that time on, every afternoon, when the officials had dispersed and the courtyard was empty, I carried a fan and paced in the back garden. Climbing the ancient city wall, I gathered lysium and chrysanthemum or pulled at the flowers and bamboos. The myriad phenomena approached me to present poetic material. Although I would wave them away, they would not leave me. Before I had time to answer those in front, the ones behind were already pressing me.[15]

The idea that, after a poet is enlightened, poetry comes to him of itself and without any special effort is forcefully expressed in a later poem of Yang's written in 1190:

Refining lines, how could I be without furnace and hammer?
Yet a line is not written entirely with these.
This old fellow doesn't hunt for the poetry;
The poetry comes hunting for him!!![16]

Thus, a poet must go through a period of "refining," but once he has passed beyond the stage of close study and learning, the creative process is completely spontaneous.

The third line of the first of two poems we have translated (p. 41) refers to the Ch'an Buddhist tradition of transmitting the master's teaching to a particularly enlightened student, symbolized by the master presenting his begging bowl and robe to the student. The most famous transmission of the robe is the secret transmission by Hung-jen (601–674) to the sixth Ch'an patriarch Hui-neng (638–713), the first master of the Southern School of Ch'an and spiritual ancestor of all later Ch'an sects in China. In line with what Yang writes about the impossibility of transmitting the method of poetry, we should mention that Hui-neng refused to transmit *his* robe to any of his disciples, claiming that "the robe may not be handed down. . . . If you depend on the meaning of the verse of the First Patriarch, Bodhidharma, then there is no need to hand down the robe."[17] The transmission of the *dharma* from teacher to student was a mystery that could not adequately be represented by the gift of a robe or begging bowl.

According to later Ch'an tradition, Buddha first transmitted the Ch'an teaching to Mahākāśyapa merely by showing a flower to his disciples, upon which Mahākāśyapa proved his sole understanding of the teaching by being the only disciple to smile. Concerning this story, the Sung monk Hui-k'ai (1184–1260), author of the *Pass Without a Gate*, says:

Yellow-faced Buddha, acting as if there were no one near him, forced good people into slavery. While hanging up a sheep's head, he sold dog meat instead, thinking all the time how marvelous this was. But if at that time everybody had smiled, then how could he have transmitted the treasure of the true *dharma* eye, or if Mahākāśyapa had not smiled, how could he have transmitted the treasure? If he says there is a transmission of the true *dharma* eye, then that yellow-faced old geezer would be cheating country bumpkins. But if he says there is no transmission, then why did he approve of Mahākāśyapa alone?[18]

Hui-k'ai agrees with Hui-neng that the Ch'an student should not become attached to any particular method or teacher, for the secrets of Ch'an cannot be transmitted in such a way.

Yang uses these ideas developed by the Ch'an Buddhists as a device to attack the thoughtless imitation of earlier poets that was so popular in his own age. Yang has already told us how he struggled in

his youth to rid himself of the influence of the Kiangsi poets, and at
this time, he was one of the few writers who was opposed to the
imitative Kiangsi style represented most prominently by Huang
T'ing-chien. From the time of Su Shih onwards, the Sung poets had
been moving away from the natural simplicity of the earlier Northern Sung poets such as Ou-yang Hsiu (1007–1072) and Mei Yao-
ch'en (1002–1060) to a more artificial poetry characterized by extensive use of literary allusion and careful polishing of the poetic line,
and the later poets set up the T'ang poet Tu Fu as a model for slavish
imitation. Huang T'ing-chien himself wrote:

> To create new words oneself is most difficult. When Tu Fu wrote poetry or
> Han Yü wrote prose, every word had its source. It is probably because later
> men read few books that they said Han or Tu created these words them-
> selves. Those men of ancient times who were skilled in literature were truly
> able to refine and smelt the myriad manifestations of the universe. They
> filled their writing brushes and ink with old talk of the ancients, and yet,
> like the magic elixir, they could touch iron and change it into gold.[19]

Thus, with the Kiangsi poets the writing of poetry became a matter
of "making the old into the new."
    To such a view of literature, Yang retorted:

> I am ashamed of those who transmit sects and schools,
> For each author has his own individual style.
> Don't rest your feet beneath Huang T'ing-chien's
>   and Ch'en Shih-tao's fence;
> Stick your head out beyond the ranks of T'ao Yüan-ming
>   and Hsieh Ling-yün![20]

This is not to say that Yang was opposed to all imitation of the
ancients. We have already seen how he achieved his own enlightenment only after studying earlier poets. In the learning stage,
it was quite permissible to set up a particular poet as one's model as
long as one did not become "attached" to that model. After Yang
Wan-li abandoned the Kiangsi poets, Huang T'ing-chien and Ch'en
Shih-tao, he imitated Wang An-shih, and in later years he preferred
Wang to other Northern Sung poets:

> On the boat the only thing to keep me alive is poetry;
> After reading the T'ang poets, I read Wang An-shih.
> It's not that this old fellow doesn't eat in the morning,
> I take Wang's short poems for breakfast![21]

Nevertheless, since one cannot become attached to Wang An-shih if one wishes to reach full enlightenment, one must pass from Wang to the T'ang poets:

> After Wang An-shih enables me to meditate and penetrate
> There still are the T'and poets—one more barrier![22]

One should even pass beyond the T'ang poets:

> First receiving instruction, I meditated under Wang An-shih,
> But in the end, I entrusted myself to the late T'ang poets,
> From them the *Airs of the States* are not far away;
> When you've grasped the mechanism, it's simple.[23]

According to the *Pass Without a Gate*, "to realize Ch'an one must pass beyond the barriers of the patriarchs."[24] Thus, Yang uses the process of Ch'an illumination obtained by the study of the Ch'an teachers as a metaphor for the similar process whereby the poet attains his own illumination through studying the teaching of one poetic master after another. The study of masters is not the final goal, for as the *Pass Without a Gate* further teaches us:

> The great Way has no gates,
> Yet thousands of roads enter it.
> Once one has penetrated this barrier,
> He walks alone between heaven and earth.[25]

When the poet has passed beyond the barrier of his masters, he, too, frees himself from his earlier imitations and creates his own individual style. As Yang himself explains: "You ask me what the *dharma* of good poetry is;/ There's no *dharma*, no bowl, and no robe!"[26] The result of Yang's distaste for becoming attached to any earlier poetic style is that he came to view the writing of poetry as a continuous process of development, and as soon as he tired of one style, he longed to move onto fresh ground. In the preface of his collection *Nan-hai chi* Yang says:

All my life I have loved to write poetry, yet although I first love my poetry, I later come to despise it. By 1162 my poetry changed, and I was delighted, but soon I despised it again. By 1170 my poetry changed again, and in 1177 it changed once more. . . . When Liu Huan of Ch'ao-yang was governor of Ch'ing-yüan county, he requested from me a so-called *Collection of the*

South Seas (*Nan-hai chi*) of four hundred poems. By the time I saw him
again in the capital, Liu asked me for it continually, and I was finally able to
give it to him. Alas! I am already old and I don't know, if I continue with my
present poetry, whether I can change it or not. Yu Mou [1127–1194] used to
say to me, "Each time your poems change, they advance." My poems may
change, but I don't know if they can still advance. Some other day when I
see this collection, will I be delighted with it or will I despise it?[27]

When in 1190 he prefaced his collection *Ch'ao-t'ien hsü chi,* Yang
wrote: "My eldest son Chang-ju showed it to the two gentlemen Fan
Ch'eng-ta and Yu Mou who thought my poetry had changed again,
although I wasn't aware of this myself."[28] Throughout Yang's work
we see a restless mind forever striving to change and never becoming attached to any particular master or style.

   The last two lines of the first critical poem we have translated
above ("In Answer to Li T'ien-lin") do not seem to make much sense
until we realize that the comparison of the flavor of true poetry to
"frosty crab" cooked in "wine dregs" refers to the famous doctrine of
"flavor beyond flavor" advanced by the late T'ang critic Ssu-k'ung
T'u (837–908). This doctrine was of great importance to later poets
and was held in high esteem by Su Shih and other Northern Sung
writers. In his "Letter to Master Li Discussing Poetry," Ssu-k'ung
T'u writes:

Prose is difficult to discuss, but poetry is even more difficult. There have
been many metaphors for this from ancient to modern times, but I think
one must be discerning in "flavor" before one can discuss poetry. In South
China there are many things which will serve as sustenance. If we consider
pickles, we cannot say that these are not sour, yet they are merely sour and
nothing more. Or in the case of brine, we cannot say it is not salty, yet it is
merely salty and nothing more. That we northerners use these things to
relieve our hunger but then immediately desist eating them is because we
know that beyond their mere saltiness and sourness, they are deficient in
what is pure and delicious. That the southerners are used to them and
cannot discriminate them from other food is understandable.[29]

Later in his letter, Ssu-k'ung T'u praises Li's knowledge of poetry by
saying that he "knows the excellence beyond flavor."
   Yang applied Ssu-k'ung T'u's concept of flavor to all scholarly
work in general:

In reading books, one must know of the flavor beyond flavor. One who does
not know the flavor beyond flavor and says he can read books is mistaken. A

poem of the *Airs of the States* states, "Who says the thistle is bitter?/ It is sweet as the shepherd's purse." I take this as my method for reading books. When one eats the bitterest thing in the world, he obtains the sweetest thing in the world. The act of eating is the same in men, but what is obtained is not the same![30]

Yang applies this concept to poetry specifically:

When we talk of poems of the Kiangsi school, the poetry is Kiangsi in style, but not all of the poets are from Kiangsi. What do I mean by "the poets are not all from Kiangsi, but the poems are Kiangsi?" I am joining them all together. With what am I joining them together? With their flavor, not their form. Su Shih said, "The mussel is like the lichee," and "Tu Fu's poems are like Ssu-ma Ch'ien's [145–ca.86 B.C.] history." Although they pretended to agree with him, those who heard these words of Su were confused then, and today people still are confused. This is not the fault of the confused, for they reject the flavor of style and discuss similarity in form, so they are naturally confused. If we speak of form and nothing more, the Kiangsi poet Kao Ho [fl. 1100] is not similar to Hsieh Yi [fl. 1077] and Hsieh K'o [fl. 1094]; the two Hsieh's are not similar to Hung P'eng [1060–1104], Hung Yen [fl. 1107], and Hung Ch'u [fl. 1106]; the three Hung's are not similar to Hsü Fu [?–1140]; and Hsü Fu is not similar to Ch'en Shih-tao and even less to Huang T'ing-chien. This is flavor and nothing more. Sourness and saltiness are combined differently, while mountain and seafood are different delicacies, but the miracle of seasoning and cooking arises from the same hand. One can seek for the similarities and differences, but one can forget them, too![31]

At first sight Ssu-k'ung T'u's and Yang Wan-li's concept of "flavor" is somewhat difficult to understand, and yet Yang's contrast of outward form with flavor gives us a hint as to what both authors meant. Generally speaking, Yang's idea of a flavor beyond form in poetry is closely akin to the Ch'an contention that ultimate truth is inexpressible in rational terms and can only be intuited. It might be objected that the poet is a prisoner of form and words, but Yang stresses that poetic form is only an external appearance and the actual "flavor" of the poem is something that can only be intuited and not rationally explained:

Then what is poetry? Some say: "It is words and nothing else." I say that one who is good at poetry does away with words. "But then it is meaning and nothing else." I say that one who is good at poetry does away with the meaning. "But when one does away with words and meaning, where is there any poetry left?" I say that when one does away with words and meaning, the poetry still exists. "But where is the poetry then?" I say, "Have you ever tasted sweets or bitter tea? Who doesn't like sweets? At first they are sweet, but in the end, they taste sour. People all complain of the bitterness of tea, but before its bitterness is exhausted, its sweetness is incomparable. Poetry, too, is just like this." Formerly when Duke Pao slandered Duke Su, Duke Su satirized him, but today, if we look at Duke Su's poem, there are no words of satire, and we cannot see the meaning of his satire. Duke Su wrote: "Two men follow each other/ Who has made this disaster?" When he caused Duke Pao to hear of this, Duke Pao thought, "He has not even referred to me, but if it isn't me, then who is it?" On the outside he didn't dare be angry, but inside, he was dying of shame.[32]

Duke Su's satire was visible in neither the words nor the meaning of his poem, and yet Duke Pao could easily "taste" the flavor of Duke Su's censure. To Yang Wan-li, good poetry is to be intuited, not rationally analyzed.

The second of the two early literary critical poems of Yang, which we translated above, is not so rich in concepts as the first, but its first line, "The *dharma* of poetry is hard for Heaven to keep secret," is derived from one of the key concepts of Ch'an Buddhism. The Ch'an school stresses that there is nothing secret about the Buddhist teachings, for once a person has lifted the veil of illusion, there is no mystery left. With regard to the supposedly secret transmission of the *dharma* from Buddha to Mahākāśyapa, the T'ang dynasty Ch'an master Tao-ying (d. 901) said: "If you don't understand, it remains a secret of the World Honored Buddha, but if you do understand, it becomes the unkept secret of Mahākāśyapa."[33] Fo-kuo (d. 1135) commented: "The Buddha had a secret, but Mahāhāśyapa did not keep it; that Mahāhāśyapa did not keep the secret was the Buddhas's real secret. What is not kept secret is a secret, but what is kept secret is not a secret."[34] When Yang Wan-li was spiritually awakened, he wrote:

Suddenly, I didn't feel the difficulty of writing poetry. It was probably because the poet's "disease" was about to leave my body. At this time, I did not feel the difficulty of writing poetry, nor did I feel the difficulty of being a magistrate. The next year on the last of the second month when my replacement came, I matched tallies with him in order to leave and tried to collect my manuscripts. Within a total of fourteen months, I had written four hundred and ninety-two poems. I have not yet dared to show them to anyone, but this year when I occupied a post as a public bureau official, my old friend Chung Chiang-chih sent a letter from the Huai River to me saying: "Recently Ching-ch'i changed governors. Formerly you had no difficulty in governing the place, but the present replacement's troubles will be ten times greater than yours. Why don't you publish your poems from Ching-ch'i?" Laughing, I copied and sent them to him.[35]

When Yi-hsüan (d. 867), the founder of the Lin-chi Sect of Ch'an Buddhism, was studying under the master Huang-po (d. ca. 850), he was beaten three times, after having asked the true meaning of the Buddha's teaching. But after he had been fully enlightened, he stated to Ta-yü (ca. 875), "There is nothing much to Buddha's teaching."[36] Similarly, to Yang Wan-li there was nothing mysterious or difficult about the writing of poetry.

One of the most striking proofs that Yang did not consider the creation of poetry to be difficult is the tremendous number of poems he wrote, over four thousand two hundred, second only to his contemporary and friend Lu Yu. When one compares this number to the generally smaller collections of individual T'ang dynasty authors, it is, indeed, a staggering figure, especially when we realize that Yang burned over a thousand of his poems written previous to 1162, when he was already thirty-five. We have seen that in 1177 Yang was greatly dismayed because he had written "only" five hundred and eighty-two poems in the fifteen years preceding his poetic enlightenment. From that time onward, Yang was deeply concerned with the quantity of his poetic production, for after he had discarded his imitation of earlier poets, he wrote four hundred and ninety-two poems in the short space of fourteen months. Yang's obsession with continual creativity remained with him throughout his life, and in the preface to his fourth collection, *Nan-hai chi*, he proudly writes: "From 1162 to the present, my poems come to more than two thousand one hundred."[37] When he was in mourning for his mother's death from 1182 to 1184, he did not write any poetry, and his eldest son, Chang-ju, must have noticed his father's restlessness, for Yang writes in his preface to the *Ch'ao-t'ien chi* (1188):

Chang-ju begged me, "Father, you have not written any poetry for a long time, so now you should write some." Somewhat startled, I said, "If for three years one does not practice ritual, then ritual will be ruined, and if for three years one does not write poems, then poetry will decay. It would be best to follow your advice." On that day I started to make a draft on the subject of the *chin-shih* examination. On the twenty-seventh I was presented a post and called to my duty. Ten days later, I started on my journey to the capital and only wrote some twenty odd poems, but I felt they were somewhat awkward and did not convey my meaning, because I probably had not forgotten my sorrow yet.[38]

Yang recovered quickly, for in a preface written in 1190 he informs us: "From the year 1162 to now, there are close to three thousand poems in all of my seven collections."[39]

Apparently, many later critics did not agree with Yang's conception of poetry as something simple for the enlightened, for some of them attacked what they considered the excessive quantity of poetry which Yang preserved in his complete works. Typical of these critics is the Ch'ing poet Yeh Hsieh (1627–1703), who wrote:

Collections of poetry and prose which emphasize quantity will inevitably be bad. The imperishable works worthy of transmission from antiquity are not so because of quantity. The few poems of Su Wu [d. 60 B.C.] and Li Ling [d. 74 B.C.] will last for a thousand ages. Men of later ages gradually prized quantity, and Yüan Chen [779–831] and Po Chü-yi [772–846], with their *Collection of the Ch'ang-ch'ing Period,* were the first to carry things too far. Within this collection that which is decadent and vulgar comprises sixty or seventy percent. If they had done away with this sixty or seventy percent, the twenty or thirty percent left would all be outstanding and famous works. Of the Sung authors rich in poems, none exceeded Yang Wan-li and Chou Pi-ta [1126–1204]. Among their compositions there is hardly one poem or even one line that can be approved. . . . If we view things this way, what use is there in quantity?[40]

Obviously, Yang's contemporaries did not agree with this view that only a poet's "masterpieces" are significant, for when Yang Wan-li showed the famous poet Yu Mou a few lines from the early poetry which he had burned, Yu Mou sighed and said, "Why should poetry be of one form only? What a shame you burned them!"[41]

From the concept of Ch'an as nothing difficult or mysterious, one can logically conclude that the activities of the enlightened man do not differ materially from those of the ordinary man. In the *Pass Without a Gate* we read: "Chao-chou (778–897) asked Nan-ch'üan (748–795), 'What is the Way like?' Nan-ch'üan replied, 'The ordinary mind is the Way.' "[42] The T'ang layman P'ang Yün (d. 808) wrote in a poem approved by his master: "Spiritual penetration and miraculous function are like carrying water and moving firewood."[43] Similarly, the poet who has reached the highest stage need not search for his themes in unusual or abstruse subjects but rather finds his topics for poetry in ordinary objects. We have already seen that when Yang had awakened, he found poetry came to him naturally while merely walking in the backyard during his spare time. One does not write poetry by locking himself in his study, and ordinary travel provides all of the themes required:

> Mountain thoughts and river feelings don't disappoint them,
> For the rain's aspect and the clear weather's appearance
>   are always wonderful.
> To close your door and hunt for lines is not the
>   method of poetry;
> When you're traveling, the lines come of themselves. [44]

Since poetry is not the result of intense effort and comes of itself through ordinary experience, the ideal poem is artless and natural. How much the love of the unadorned was the influence of Ch'an Buddhism or of even more ancient tendencies of the Chinese is difficult to say, but Yang himself had a strong appreciation for the simple and unadorned. Yang's description of a small rural inn he stopped at during one of his travels is typical:

> I get off my palanquin and find a new inn;
> I open its door, arriving at a small side room.
> Inside there's a single yew table,
> And two rush mats facing one another.
> The rafter bamboos are green, joints remaining;
> The eaves' rushes white, still bearing roots.
> I have only one regret about the white window—
> Where its papers were joined, there still is a scar. [45]

Everything in the small room is completely natural except for the scar left by gluing papers together to make a window pane.

Such an ordinary activity as sunning his clothes made Yang write:

> At high noon I sun my clothes, in the afternoon fold
>   them up;
> I carry them back home in a cloth-covered willow basket.
> My wife and children laugh and ask each other:
> "Who in the world is that bare-footed servant over there?" [46]

Few government officials of Yang's period would have liked to think of themselves as being on the same level as common servants even in jest, but Yang's poem is completely in harmony with the idea that one can be a creative poet even while living in complete simplicity and naturalness.

However, many of Yang's contemporaries did not agree with his love of simplicity in poetry, and the entire Kiangsi group, against which Yang had revolted in his youth, stood diametrically opposed to Yang's artlessness. In two poems written in praise of the Northern Sung poet Chang Lei (1052–1112), Yang both criticized the attitude of Huang T'ing-chien, leader of the Kiangsi school, and also advanced his theory of the naturalness of good verse:

> In front of Huang T'ing-chien, Chang Lei dared to
>   speak of poetry,
> And Huang highly praised his lines "rinsing the well,"
>   "sweeping flowers."
> If later, someone had made Huang read his complete works;
> Huang would have found another *natural* treasure, but
>   what did Huang know of such things![47]

Yang's point is that Huang and his group of Kiangsi poets only knew enough to praise a particularly clever turn of phrase or usage of words, but that they were incapable of understanding the "natural treasure" of Chang's poetry. That Yang meant Chang's artlessness by "natural treasure" is made even clearer in the first of the two poems:

> Lately I've come to love the Fat Immortal's poetry
>   for being so natural;
> He never embroidered or painted, much less carved or
>   engraved.
> Spring flowers, autumn moon, the winter's ice and snow;
> I never hear stale words from him, I just hear nature![48]

In other words, Chang Lei chose his themes from the natural objects around him and did not engage in gathering stale words from old books and stringing them together with rhymes.

III   *Yang Wan-li and Yen Yü*

Among the poets and critics inspired by Ch'an ideas after Yang Wan-li, the most significant was Yen Yü (fl. 1180–1235), author of the highly influential work on literary theory entitled *Ts'ang-lang shih-hua*, or *Ts'ang-lang's Poetry Talks*. Yen considered Yang Wan-li one of the most important poets of Chinese literature and honors him by including his poetry as one of the major styles (*t'i*) of Chinese verse. In his description of Yang's poetry, Yen repeats what Yang has already told us about his process of enlightenment: "At first he studied Wang An-shih and Ch'en Shih-tao, and finally he studied short poems from the T'ang authors. At last, he abandoned the forms of the various poets and produced his own 'mechanism.' "[49]

Although Yen Yü does not acknowledge any debt to Yang Wan-li's views on literature, there is much in common between them, and direct influence should not be ruled out. About the necessity for enlightenment, Yen says:

> In general, the way of Ch'an lies in miraculous enlightenment, and the way of poetry also lies in miraculous enlightenment. The power of Meng Hao-jan's [689–740] learning was far below that of Han Yü [768–824], but the reason his poetry went beyond Han Yü's was entirely due to his miraculous enlightenment. Only enlightenment is the vocation and basic type.[50]

Yen also agreed with Yang in criticizing the artificiality and formalism of the Kiangsi poets:

> At the beginning of this dynasty, poetry still followed the T'ang style. . . . But when Su Shih and Huang T'ing-chien first gave expression to their own ideas in the making of poems, the T'ang style was altered; Huang T'ing-chien was particularly forced in his labors. After that, their rules flourished, and all within the seas called them the Kiangsi school.[51]

Another point on which Yang Wan-li and Yen Yü agreed is the necessity of studying the great poets of the past in order to arrive at the stage where sudden enlightenment can occur: "Finally, one chooses widely from the famous poets of the Flourishing T'ang and 'ferments' them in his breast, and after a long time he is naturally enlightened. . . . This is called 'the sudden gate' or 'entering straight with a single sword.' "[52]

Yen Yü was one of the first critics to put so much stress on the Flourishing T'ang, the so-called "golden age" of T'ang poetry. We shall see that Yang Wan-li was much more deeply indebted to the late T'ang poets than to Yen Yü's masters, Li Po and Tu Fu. The difference in poetic preferences between Yang and Yen is of fairly minor importance, but it is associated with a profound difference between their views regarding the process by which sudden enlightenment is to be obtained. Yang held that imitation is allowable and even necessary, but that the poet should view the object of imitation as merely a barrier (*kuan*) which is to be passed when he reaches a certain degree of enlightenment. Yang certainly had preferences for individual poets, but he never attempted to fit the poetic creations of Chinese literature into a rigid hierarchy as Yen Yü does:

> In the Ch'an school, there are a Great and Small Vehicle, a north and south sect, and a heterodox and orthodox path. Those who study must follow the highest vehicle and realize the correct *dharma* eye, and, thus, be enlightened to the Supreme Truth. The fruits of the *śrāvaka* and the *pratyeka-buddha* are not orthodox. Discussing poetry is like discussing Ch'an. The poetry of Han, Wei, Chin, and Flourishing T'ang are the Supreme Truth. The poems from the Ta-li period [766–780] onward are Small Vehicle Ch'an, and they have already fallen into the second truth. The poems of the Late T'ang are the fruit of the *śrāvaka* and *pratyeka-buddha*. Studying the poetry of Han, Wei, and Flourishing T'ang, one is in the Lin-chi sect; studying the poetry from after Ta-li, one is in the Ts'ao-tung sect.[53]

Yang Wan-li strongly emphasized that each author has his own style which sets him apart as an individual, and, thus, he would have found a rigid division of poets into various sects extremely distasteful. As he had said: "I am ashamed of those who transmit sects and schools."[54]

Yang Wan-li had first studied his near contemporaries, the Kiangsi school, and only then moved on to imitate the authors of T'ang times. There does not seem to have been any particular design in this movement from modern to more ancient authors, but Yen Yü set up a definite chronological order in which the aspiring poet should study the authors of the past:

> In studying poetry, you ought to make understanding the principal thing. In entering the gate, you must be correct, and in setting your goals, you must be lofty. . . . First you must read *Songs of the South* thoroughly, reciting it morning and night as your foundation; then read the *Nineteen Ancient Poems* and the four Music Bureau poems. The five-character poems of Li Ling and Su Wu and those of the Han and Wei dynasties must all be thoroughly read. Then you must peruse the collected works of Li Po and Tu Fu again and again, just as modern men memorize the Confucian classics. Later, choose widely from the famous masters of the Flourishing T'ang and "ferment" them in your breast, and, after a long time, you will be naturally

enlightened. Although you may not be successful in your study, at least you will not lose the correct path.[55]

The Ch'ing critic Yeh Hsieh violently attacked this aspect of Yen Yü's literary criticism with arguments that Yang Wan-li would have seconded:

When Yen Yü says that in studying poetry one should be understanding, he is correct. When one has understanding, he can then spread out before himself the poetry of the Han, Wei, and Six Dynasties, along with the complete poems of T'ang and Sung. Then he will certainly be able to know by himself what should be chosen and what is reliable, which is called "trusting the hand to pick out nothing that is not the Way." But if one then speaks of Han, Wei, and the Flourishing T'ang, even a five-foot boy or a village tutor of three families has been skilled in teaching and learning such things for a long time. This is like a great thoroughfare to which the masses throng in hordes, for even a blind man is able to follow them. Why must a person wait for understanding before he can do that? I think that if he does not have understanding, then even if he hastens step by step after the Han, Wei, and Flourishing T'ang, there is no place without poetry demons. If he does have understanding, then even if he does not hurry in the footsteps of Han, Wei, and Flourishing T'ang, all poetry demons will turn into supreme knowledge, and no harm will be done to Han, Wei, and Flourishing T'ang. How misleading and perverse was this talk of Yen Yü and how contradictory was his thought![56]

A comparison of Yang Wan-li's and Yen Yü's theories of literature shows a profound contrast between the two critics and helps to bring Yang's contribution to Chinese literary theory into sharper focus for us. For Yang Wan-li, the major fault of Yen Yü would not lie in his selection of masters, but that he did not transcend his masters, remaining attached to them. Yen Yü did not understand the true spirit of Ch'an, and in this respect Yen Yü was Hīnayāna and Yang Wan-li Mahāyāna.

CHAPTER 3

The Live Method

I Background

IN the second of two short poems presented to Yang Wan-li in the year 1189, Yang's friend Chang Tzu (ca. 1195) wrote:

> There is no end to the spirit of your creativity;
> With leaps and bounds, you race on quickly as possible.
> I don't know how many of your works lie before my eyes,
> But poems with your "live method" are rare.[1]

At about the same time, another friend, Chou Pi-ta, wrote to him: "In all things, Yang Wan-li has been enlightened to the 'live method.' "[2]

Ever since Chang Tzu and Chou Pi-ta praised Yang Wan-li's mastery of the live method (huo-fa), critics have considered it to be the basis of his claim to originality in the Chinese poetic tradition, and in his introduction to Yang Wan-li's poetry, the twentieth-century scholar Chou Ju-ch'ang focuses most of his attention on Yang's live method.[3] However, Yang's immediate contemporaries were not the first critics to speak of the live method, and by late Northern Sung times, the critic of the Kiangsi school, Lü Pen-chung, stressed the importance of the live method:

> Studying poetry, you must understand the live method. What is meant by live method is that all of the rules are observed but you are able to transcend the rules; that is to say, the changes and transformations in the poetry are unfathomable, yet you do not turn your back on the rules. This Path has a set method, yet it is without a set method. It lacks a set method yet it possesses a set method. If someone understands this, then you can discuss the live method with him.[4]

Although Lü Pen-chung's use of the term "live method" may be slightly different from that of Yang's contemporaries, they would agree on the essential meaning, as we can see from Liu K'o-chuang's (1187–1269) statement on this matter: "Later Yang Wan-li appeared, and he really obtained the so-called live method, that is to say, rolling and perfect like a small pill. I regret that Lü Pen-chung was not able to see him."[5]

Liu K'o-chuang lived in the generation following Yang Wan-li and his friends Chang Tzu and Chou Pi-ta, so Liu's comments concerning the live method help us to define what the commonly accepted meaning of the term was from the times of Lü Pen-chung down to the end of the Sung dynasty. One of the most important points in common between Lü Pen-chung's and Liu K'o-chuang's description of the live method is the reference to some form of constant, dynamic motion, for Lü refers to "changes and transformations" while Liu speaks of the poetry as "rolling and perfect like a small pill." We have already examined Yang's continuous obsession with transforming the style of his poetry, but we shall find the idea of change and, particularly, unexpected change, to be a fundamental concept which underlies all of his verse.

Liu K'o-chuang's comments do not enlighten us much further about the meaning of the term "live method," but Lü Pen-chung tells us more, though unfortunately not as much as one might wish. The most striking feature of Lü's description of the live method is the paradoxical language in which it is couched. One observes the rules, while transcending them. There is a path for the live method, but there is no path. Although such pronouncements seem quite vague on first sight, the use of paradoxical language strongly resembles many of Yang Wan-li's statements about the nature of poetry, which we have examined above. Thus, when asked about the *dharma* of good poetry, Yang replied: "There's no *dharma*, no bowl, and no robe." When discussing the elements of poetry, Yang has told us that "one who is good at poetry does away with words but emphasizes the meaning and nothing more. Further, one who is good at poetry does away with the meaning."

Although it is impossible to state specifically the points of contact between Lü Pen-chung's description of the live method and Yang Wan-li's theory of literature, the use of paradox in both cases makes clear the influence of Ch'an mysticism. The term "live method," or *huo-fa*, itself suggests Buddhist influence, for in interpreting Sung literary critical terms, we should always be conscious of the ambiguity of the word *fa*, which can retain its common secular meanings of "method," "law," or can be used to translate the Sanskrit term *dharma* with such a wide range of meanings as "Buddhist law or path" and even "constituent elements of being." Sung critics constantly played on the ambiguity of such words, and we have frequently found occasions in which it was necessary to translate *fa* as *dharma*, in order to make the Buddhist connotations of the word clearer.

We are fortunate that a friend of Yang Wan-li, Ko T'ien-min, leaves no doubt about the connection between Yang's live method and Ch'an Buddhism in a poem he sent to Yang:

Meditating on Ch'an and studying poetry are not two different *dharmas* (*fa*);
Yang understands how to make a dead snake leap with life.
With spirit upright, mind empty, his eyes transcend of themselves;
His fur-cutting sword, though unmoving, can either spare or kill.
His live mechanism does not avoid the common language;
In recent ages only Yang Wan-li has been like this.[6]

A diligent search of Sung dynasty Ch'an texts has failed to locate the term "live method," so it probably was invented by Lü Pen-chung; yet such writers as Ko T'ien-min clearly saw the connection between Lü's live method and Ch'an Buddhism. What makes Ch'an and the live method "alive" is that both reject all "grasping" at objects. We have already seen that Yang Wan-li's theory of literature rejects attachment to earlier literary models. Similarly, the Ch'an monk strives to liberate his mind by refusing to become attached to his teachers or any particular set of dogma. However, the detachment of the Ch'an adept and the practitioner of the live method is even broader in scope than a mere rejection of previous models, for both the monk and poet refuse to become attached to any object whatsoever. Just as the Ch'an master frees himself from the cycle of birth and death by his lack of attachment to things, the writer who practices the live method is constantly "on the move." In the words of Lü Pen-chung, his "changes and transformations are unfathomable," for "the Path has a set method, yet it is without a set method."

The absence of grasping in the live method of Yang Wan-li and the Ch'an monk is connected to one of the most fundamental ideas of Mahayana Buddhism, namely, nondualism. This concept was developed formally by the Indian Buddhist philosopher Nagārjuna in his *Madhyamaka-śāstra,* which became the basis for most later Buddhist thought in India, China, and Tibet: "Nothing disappears, nothing appears, nothing has an end, nothing is eternal./Nothing is identical to itself, nor different; nothing moves, to or fro."[7] In such a nondualistic system all distinctions between subject and object were obliterated, and, hence, grasping was completely impossible. The ultimate path to liberation was elimination of dualisms, and thus both Lü Pen-chung and Yang Wan-li used Nagārjuna's form of paradox in their descriptions of the live method, for only in paradox are distinctions destroyed.

By now the reader may feel somewhat mystified as to the exact significance of the term "live method," and, indeed, we would find the Sung dynasty critics's explanation of live method nearly impossible to comprehend if it were not for the many concrete examples of the method to be found in Yang Wan-li's own poetry. Thus, we should now proceed to the poems themselves in order to understand what Yang's contemporaries found "live" about them. Although none of the ancient critics who dealt with Yang Wan-li enumerated the basic elements of Yang's live method, we have seen fit to treat the method under the following topics: (1) iconoclasm, (2) illusionistic and paradoxical language, (3) surprise and sudden enlightenment, (4) humor, and (5) colloquial language. We can never be sure that Sung critics would have included all of these elements under the rubric of live method, but we feel that these are the most important devices by which Yang Wan-li prevents his poetry from falling into a dualistic "dead method" and thereby keeps it continuously on the move.

II *Iconoclasm*

One of the most important elements of Yang Wan-li's live method is hinted at in a short poem written soon after his poetical enlightenment:

Light Rain

Lonely, depressed, speechless, I lean against my door;
Plum flowers, light rain, it's almost dusk.
What a shame the eaves' raindrops aren't open-minded;
Drip, drip, when did they ever leave their old rut?[8]

Yang felt that the majority of poets contemporary with him were in a "rut" just as raindrops dripping from eaves, and throughout his

Poetry Talks he constantly praises those poets who were able to
overthrow the accepted traditions of their own ages:

> In T'ang regulated poetry there are seven characters for each of eight lines,
> and in any poem, each line is unusual, each word is unusual. . . . For
> example, Tu Fu writes in his poem on the Ninth Day . . . : "I am ashamed
> with such short hair to have my hat blown off/ So I laughingly ask someone
> next me to straighten my cap." In writing this couplet, he has overturned
> something, for Meng Chia considered his hat falling off to be romantic, but
> Tu Fu considered it not falling off to be romantic. Tu Fu has overturned all
> of the "public cases" of ancient men, which is his most miraculous method.[9]

What Yang Wan-li admires most in Tu Fu is his unconventional
attitude toward the tradition of poetry he had inherited in the T'ang
dynasty. Even before he had fully rejected his earlier master, Yang
enjoyed making fun of previously accepted stereotypes:

I Gaze at the Moon on a Frosty Night from my Study "Snow Angling Boat"

I stand a bit by the creekside, waiting for the moon impatiently,
But the moon knows my intentions, and comes out late on purpose.
I go home and close my doors, so depressed, I don't look for her,
When suddenly she flies over the tips of a thousand peaks.
I climb to Snow Angling Boat and watch her a while;
Her icy wheel just hangs there on a pine tree's branch.
"Does the poet prefer the moon now or at the mid-autumn festival?"[10]
Someone asks, but I just shake my head.
All year long, it's only in December that the moon's color
Is rubbed and polished in snow juice, washed in frosty water.
In all eight directions for ten thousand miles there's only one blue sky,
And her white jade platter floats out over this azure lake.
Moreover, she invites the plum flowers to be her companions;
Doesn't the mid-autumn festival lack all of *this*?[11]

From early T'ang times at least, the mid-autumn festival was
considered the most appropriate time for viewing the moon, but
when someone expresses this traditional viewpoint, Yang merely
shakes his head in disgust, and then proceeds to point out why the
moon is a much more splendid sight in the twelfth month. This early
poem of Yang Wan-li is obviously no revolutionary break with
Chinese literary tradition, but the unconventionality we see here in
an embryonic form would later give rise to Yang's rejection of many

of the timeworn stereotypes of Chinese poetry, as we shall find in later chapters.

We shall defer our discussion of the more original elements in Yang Wan-li's verse until later and limit ourselves here to a study of one of the iconoclastic devices used in Yang's works, namely, *fan-an*, or "turning over the case." What this term means can be seen from a section in his *Poetry Talks* where Yang praises earlier poets who used the same method:

When Confucius [552–479 B.C.] and Lao-tzu [sixth century B.C.?] saw one another, they lowered the covers of their chariots, so Tsou Yang [ca. 206–129 B.C.] wrote: "They lowered the chariot covers as if they were old friends." Sun Mou [11th. cent.] and Su Shih did not know each other, so when Sun sent him a poem, Su Shih answered: "I don't need to lower my chariot cover for you!" When Liu K'uan was an official, he made a whip of reeds, because he was so lenient. Su Shih wrote: "I have a whip I don't use, so who needs reeds?" Tu Fu wrote: "I suddenly recall the ruins by an autumn well/ The white bones of ancient men were covered with green moss/ How could a man not drink and make his heart sad?" Su Shih wrote: "Why must you wait for the ruins by an autumn well/ And hold a wine cup, *only* when you see men's white bones?" These are all examples of the method of "turning over the case."[12]

From Yang's discussion it should be clear that *fan-an* is a poetical device by which a poet turns the language and ideas of an earlier poet upside down. It is also significant that all of the examples of *fan-an* which Yang gives come from the work of Su Shih, the great Northern Sung master who was largely responsible for the revolution in Sung dynasty poetry.

Examples of *fan-an* are legion in Yang's own work, but since this form of verbal iconoclasm is difficult to appreciate outside of the original language, let us just cite a few lines. In his famous poem "Drinking Alone Beneath the Moon" Li Po had written: "The moon doesn't know how to drink."[13] Yang Wan-li retorts: " 'The moon doesn't know how to drink' is really reckless talk!"[14] In the same poem Li Po's moon is totally aloof from the poet, but Yang Wan-li writes: "I chant and the moon knows how to listen."[15] In his *Proclamation of North Mountain*, K'ung Chih-kuei (447–501) described the creatures of the wilderness which are upset because a recluse has abandoned his mountain hermitage: "His orchid curtains empty, the night cranes complain/ The mountain man has gone, the morn-

ing apes are frightened."[16] When Yang Wan-li decides to retire from
his official career after having viewed some particularly magnificent
scenery, he writes: "I'm tired of wandering and ought to go home/
And not just because of the apes' and cranes' complaint!"[17] When he
was drunk Li Po had written: "Jade Mountain falls over by itself,
without anyone pushing."[18] Under similar circumstances Yang
Wan-li writes: "Who gives a damn whether Jade Mountain falls over
or not?"[19] In all such cases Yang Wan-li is gleefully turning the most
famous lines of the most revered authors upside down.

In his discussion of Tu Fu's iconoclasm above, Yang Wan-li stated
that Tu Fu had "overturned all of the 'public cases' of ancient
men. . . ." The term "public cases," or *kung-an* (Japanese *kō-an*), is
taken directly from Ch'an literature, and it is very likely that Yang's
use of *fan-an*, or "turning over the case," was inspired by Sung
dynasty Ch'an practices. Just as Tu Fu and Su Shih turned over
"public cases" of earlier poetry masters, the Sung author of the *Pass
Without a Gate* turned the "public case" of the earlier T'ang dynasty
Ch'an master Nan-ch'üan upside down: "Nan-ch'üan said: 'The
mind is not the Buddha, and knowledge is not the Way.' I say:
'Nan-ch'üan did not know shame because he was getting old, and so
opened his stinking mouth, exposing his family scandal to outsid-
ers. . . .' "[20] The reason why our author is so violent toward Nan-
ch'üan is not because he is in disagreement with the T'ang master's
doctrine, but because a Ch'an monk must overturn all of his masters
in order to attain the freedom of enlightenment. Nan-ch'üan's public
case can serve as an object of meditation in the beginning stages, but
eventually even such concepts as "the mind is not the Buddha" must
be discarded. Similarly, the practice of *fan-an* is one means by
which Yang Wan-li could transcend the masters of T'ang and earlier
poetry. Iconoclasm destroys the dualistic relation between master
and student, which the original poet must transcend to attain life.

III   *Illusionistic and Paradoxical Language*

In another chapter we shall discuss Yang Wan-li's fascination with
optical illusions as part of his Buddhist philosophical interests. On
the level of poetic technique, the use of illusionistic language is one
of the most important elements in his live method. In the following
poem we can observe how Yang creates a whole series of illusions
through the use of such language:

Making Fire in the Boat on a Snowy Day

Raven silver [charcoal] catches fire and gives forth green fog,[21]
So I pretend it's a large stick of heavy aloes incense.
Stopping, then starting, it billows forth thickly;
Scattered into a fine mist, it warms my robe and trousers.
But in a moment the fog clears, spitting out red rays,
And blazes like the rising sun on cloud surfaces.
This bright spring, mild sun warm my whole room;
My pale face reddens; I think I'm in the Land of Drunks!
Suddenly the fire grows cold, and the fog all disappears;
All I see is snowy [ash] piled up in my red stove.
Outside my window the snow is more than three feet deep,
But this snow inside my window is only one inch fragrant![22]

In the very first line of the poem Yang creates two illusions, for he does not simply state that the charcoal has caught fire and given forth smoke but rather that "raven silver" has ignited and produced "green fog." The illusion is continued in the second line, for now the silver/charcoal has been transformed into a stick of incense, but instead of billowing forth smoke, the "incense" proceeds to produce "mist" in the third and fourth lines. The fire born in the silver/charcoal/incense is not really fire but the rising sun, which gives rise to springlike weather in Yang's boat cabin, despite the fact that the poem is being written on a snowy day. Even the poet himself is not free from illusory transformations, for when he feels the warmth of the sun/fire, his face turns red and he is intoxicated, although he has not drunken any wine. Suddenly the illusion disappears, when the fire goes out, but in the meantime the silver/charcoal/incense has further transformed itself into snow. Even measurements of length and depth do not have any meaning in Yang's world of illusion, for the one inch of "snow" in Yang's stove is equivalent to the three feet of snow outside his window. Finally, unlike ordinary snow, this "snow," a product of fire and heat, also possesses the property of fragrance. Thus, through a series of rapidly shifting metaphors, Yang has created an illusory world quite separate from our world of normal experience.

The kinds of transformations produced by Yang's use of illusionistic language remind one of the contention of the Indian Buddhist *prajñā sūtras* that all phenomenal existence is like a sleight of hand or a mirage. In fact, Yang himself frequently compares the illusory transformation of physical objects to a magical trick played by some immortal:

Clearing Snow
(First Poem of Two)

An immortal cuts water into flying flowers;
When he changes these into jasper, it's already a miracle,
But he changes the jasper back into water,
Which, dripping to the ground, is always glass.[23]

In four short lines we see an immortal change water into flowers (snow flakes), then jasper (sleet), back into water (rain), and finally glass (standing pools of water). In short, Yang's use of illusionistic language is similar to the way the Buddhas and gods create the illusion of *māyā* in Indian Buddhist texts.

Not only is the method by which the magical transformations are effected similar to what one finds in Buddhist texts, but the very illusionistic language which Yang employs is practically identical to that of these texts. If one examines the large body of poetry which Yang wrote on the theme of transformation, he will find that words for gems and precious metals such as "jade," "jasper," "crystal," "glass," "silver," and "pearl" occupy the first place in the magical changes he describes. Anyone who has read a reasonable quantity of Indian Buddhist literature will recognize the similarity between the bejewelled world of illusion in Yang Wan-li's poetry and the same world found in practically every Indian *sūtra*. The *Lotus Sūtra* describes the Buddha field of a future Buddha in the following terms: "The ground will be made of glass with jewel trees in rows. There will be ropes of gold in order to mark the boundaries of roads. Jewel flowers will be scattered, covering everything in their purity."[24] However, in many cases, Yang Wan-li's use of such illusionistic language goes one step beyond the ornate illusory world of Indian Buddhist literature:

River Water

The water's color is originally pure white,
But, piled deeply, it turns to green.
What kind of potion did the River Fairy use
To soften this thousand miles of jade?[25]

Rather than comparing the river water to jade, Yang Wan-li surprises the reader by stating that the water only became water after the "jade" of the river was magically "softened" by an immortal. Yang uses a similar technique in a poem about the moon:

On the Night of the Twelfth of the Eighth Month I Gaze at the Moon from Sincere Study[26]

> Nearing mid-autumn, the moon is already pure;
> A circle of ice, it hangs on a raven black curtain.
> Suddenly I discover that tonight the moon
> Isn't really glued to the sky; it moves entirely on its own![27]

Yang's description of the moon as "a circle of ice" and the sky as a "raven black curtain" corresponds with his more usual type of illusory metaphor, but the last line of the poem is as unexpected as the transformation of jade into water in the preceding work. The poet obviously knows that the moon/ice is not "glued" on the sky/curtain, so when he tells the reader he is surprised by the moon moving "entirely on its own," the reader is taken off guard, just as he was when he discovered that the water of the river was originally jade.

By now, it should be reasonably clear how Yang Wan-li's use of illusionistic language fits in with his live method. We have seen that Ko T'ien-min thought that anyone with a command of the live method "understands how to make a dead snake leap with life," and Yang's illusionistic language accomplishes exactly this goal. In reading Yang Wan-li's poetry, one can never precisely determine what is "real" and what is "illusory." Plain charcoal transforms itself into silver, incense, and snow, while water can take any form ranging from jasper to glass. Hence, the reader is constantly finding himself taken aback as one illusion shifts into another, just as he would be if a dead snake suddenly stirred and leapt at him. These constant transformations breathe life into the poetry, avoiding the grasping that arises from attachment.

In addition to using illusionistic language, Buddhist *sūtras* frequently employ paradoxical language. Thus, in many Mahāyāna works one finds such expressions as "the hair of a tortoise" or "the child of a barren woman" in constant use. Such paradoxical language consists of elements which seem to be self-contradictory on the level of worldly truth and, therefore, shock the mind from its normal

thought processes to attain a nondualistic level of consciousness
where all such paradoxes are resolved.

Although paradoxical language is less common in Chinese poetry
than in Buddhist philosophical discourse, one discovers that Yang
Wan-li frequently writes such sentences as: "There is a dream, but
there never was a dream/It seems like thought, but it is not
thought."[28] Although such lines sound as if they could have been
quoted from some Buddhist text on logic, Yang Wan-li achieves
interesting effects when he applies paradoxical language to a landscape description:

Written While on the Road to Wan-an
(First Poem of Three)

Jade-peak clouds, scraped, let slanting light through;
Flower-path mud, dried; I can go out for my evening walk.
Mild, mild, a constant breeze, warm in the midst of cold;
From time to time, a few drops, rain in clear weather.[29]

In Yang's paradoxical landscape, there is heat when it is cold and
rain when the sky is clear.

However, we need not worry about the seeming contradictions in
Yang Wan-li's landscapes, for no such contradictions exist in the
realm of absolute truth. In most poems Yang resolves the contradictions which his use of paradoxical language seems to create:

Looking at the Snow on a Moon-lit Night
(Second Poem of Three)

The moon's light and the snow's color are both pure and cold; '
When I see the moon, I first suspect it's a circle of snow.
Yet I can see that the snow's light is like a moon;
In the end, the snow and moon are just the same![30]

At first the poet cannot decide whether the moon is snow or the
snow is the moon, but after musing about the seeming contradiction
between the two, he realizes their identity.

A similar resolution of a contradictory situation occurs in a landscape poem:

On the Third Day of the First Month I Spend the Night at the Village of the
Fan Clan
(First Poem of Four)

. . . .
Where did these three mountain peaks come from?
They gallop over to me like neighing colts.
By my window, they can't stand to leave;
Hesitating, they stay just for me.
Facing each other, we become four friends;
I call for wine, and let them help themselves.
I am drunk, but the mountains are sober;
We forget, yet seek, for one another.[31]

In his state of intoxication, Yang Wan-li is separate from the "sober"
mountains, and, hence, Yang and the mountains seem to forget
about one another despite their initial friendship. Yet in a
philosophical system such as Ch'an Buddhism, where one attains
enlightenment by not seeking it, there is no contradiction in Yang
and the mountains forgetting and seeking one another at the same
time.

Yang Wan-li does not use paradoxical language in his poetry as
commonly as he uses illusionistic language, but the effect is similar.
Paradox keeps the mind off balance, and brings life to what other-
wise might be dead.

IV *Sudden Enlightenment*

The problem of reality and illusion is one of the most important
themes of Yang Wan-li's poetry, and we have seen how his live
method utilizes illusionistic and paradoxical language to emphasize
the illusory nature of sense perception. Yet, when we finally realize
that our senses have been fooled into confusing illusion for reality,
our minds are startled into awareness, a process akin to that of the
man who attains sudden enlightenment after groping around in the
darkness for many years.

Such experiences of "sudden enlightenment" are frequently encountered in Yang Wan-li's poetry. While looking at some flowers,
Yang was startled to discover that some of the flowers were actually
butterflies when the "flowers" flew away:

As I look up toward the trellis, I can only see a few
  flowers from afar;
But after going upstairs, I gaze down and they stand
  out beautifully.
There's no way to distinguish the *t'u-mi* flowers from
  butterflies;[32]
Only when they fly away do you know they're not flowers![33]

A similar "awakening" occurred when Yang was watching clouds
shaped like mountain peaks in the sky:

A clear sky just before dawn, not yet light;
My eyes are full of strange peaks, always attractive.
But when one of the peaks suddenly grows,
Only then do I know, not moving, it's a *real* mountain![34]

A common method used by Ch'an masters to enlighten their
students was to shock their minds and bodies into awareness. This
frequently took the form of shouting at the student or beating him
on the body, and sometimes even more drastic methods were used
when warranted:

Whenever there was an inquiry, the monk Chü-chih [mid-ninth century]
only raised his finger in answer. Later, an outsider asked Chü-chih's boy
attendant, "What are the fundamentals of your master's teachings?" The
boy, too, merely raised his finger. Chü-chih heard of this and cut off the
boy's finger with a knife. The boy then ran away screaming and crying in
pain, but Chü-chih called him back, and when the boy turned his head
around, Chü-chih raised his finger. The boy was suddenly enlightened.[35]

We find a similar shock method employed in Yang Wan-li's
poetry, which frequently startles us into sudden enlightenment
through its unexpected changes. Prior to Yang's time, most Chinese
verse was written with careful attention to the logical order of the
poem from first line to last. Even such an innovative critic and poet
as Lü Pen-chung, who discovered the live method, wrote:
"Whenever you write poetry, you must cause people to know there
is a second line after reading the first line, and a third line after
reading the second line. Only if this order is maintained to the end
of the poem, can it considered to be wonderful."[36]

Here again, Yang did not follow traditional practice, and unexpected shifts in his poems were noticed by the late Ch'ing critic Ch'en Yen (1856–1937): "In other poems there is only one "fold," merely one twist or turn and no more. Yang Wan-li has at least two twists and turns. Other people "fold" first to the left and then "fold" further to the left. Yang Wan-li first "folds" to the left and then "folds" again to the left, but after three "folds" he finally goes to the right."[37] In his *Poetry Talks*, Yang admired similar qualities in earlier poets: "There are poems which express three ideas in one line of seven characters. Tu Fu wrote: 'Facing my food, I eat for a while, but finally cannot continue.' Han Yü wrote: 'I am going to go, but before I arrive, I think of returning.' "[38]

In Yang's own poetry, we frequently find ourselves whirling around with our ordinary sense of direction lost due to some surprise:

> The oarsmen just let the boat follow the current,
> Making no plans about water and rocks in the rapids ahead.
> A surprise torrent whirls us around three times.
> So our boat's tail becomes its head![39]

We would not be so surprised if the boat turned about merely once, but just when it seems to be returning to normal, we are startled by being swung around once more, racing down a treacherous rapids backward!

In his *Poetry Talks* Yang Wan-li praises earlier poets who succeeded in shocking the reader into a new awareness:

Some poems have lines which startle you. In his "Screen with a Landscape Painting," Tu Fu wrote: "There shouldn't be maple trees in this hall/ How strange! Rivers and mountains give rise to smoke and mist!" Also: "If you chop down the cassia tree on the moon/The moon's pure rays will be even brighter!" Po Chü-yi wrote: "From afar I pity the moon's cassia flowers for being so lonely/ So I ask if the Moon Beauty Huan-o is really there./ The moon has always had a lot of unused land,/ So why doesn't she plant two more cassia trees in its middle?"[40]

However, Yang Wan-li's shock method is much more extreme than any of the earlier examples which he cites, for Yang delights in making us imagine that something is what it is not, and then in the final line of the poem, he smashes the illusion he has created:

A young boy removes morning ice from his metal bowl,
Hanging the ice on a colored string, he makes it a silver gong.
As he strikes it a jade chime resounds throughout the woods,
When suddenly—the tinkle of glass shatters on the ground![41]

As soon as Yang has made us believe that the piece of ice is a silver
gong with the resonance of jade chimes, he smashes our dream
against the ground, but even then, the sound is that of breaking
glass and not ice!

Just as Yang smashes our dream chimes, so he enjoys shocking us
out of other dreams which he conjures up for us with his poetic
imagination:

The Boatman Plays a Flute

The Long River is windless, the water, level, green;
There are neither shoe leather wrinkles nor even gauze ripples.
As I gaze east and west, this light seems to float in the void,
Gleaming like a faultless jade for a thousand acres.
The boys in our boat can't stand being idle,
So they drunkenly pick up the flute and play midst
    clouds and haze.
With one note, pure and long, it resounds, piercing the heavens—
Like a mountain ape crying at the moon, a spring falling
    in a torrent.
Then they beat their small sheepskin hip-drum,
Heads erect like a green mountain peak, hands falling like
    raindrops.
Suddenly, in midstream, one gigantic fish
Leaps over a yard and smashes the water glass![42]

The first ten lines of the poem evoke a dream world of exquisite
beauty. We are not sitting still on land but drifting at ease in a boat
on the water midst fog and clouds, hence, with no sense of direction
or time. As if the intoxication of wine were not enough, we are
further intoxicated by the music of the flute, which does not sound
like an ordinary flute but is "a mountain ape crying at the moon," or
the waters of a torrential spring. Suddenly, this idyll is shattered by
a huge fish coming from beneath the mysterious waters, and we are
shocked out of our dream into the world of reality.

Sometimes, rather than startle us into awareness by shattering a
dream world he has created for us, Yang chooses the method of

driving us back into a corner and just when we expect to be relieved, delivers a blow to us stronger than anything before:

Spending the Night at the River-Port Pool Rock

At the third watch, no moon, the sky's really black;
A flash of lightning is followed by the roar of thunder.
Rain pierces the sky, falling on my boat-hut's roof;
A driving wind blows across, crooked, then straight.
The loose matting leaks, soaking my bedding;
The sound of waves beats my pillow, a paper's width away.
In the middle of dreams, I am startled awake and can't
    sleep.
Grabbing my clothes, I sit up straight and sigh over and over.
I have experienced every difficulty and hardship during
    my travels,
But in my whole life there's been nothing like tonight!
Lord Heaven scares me with his nasty jokes;
Without informing me, he gave me this surprise.
He may not be able to suddenly gather his wind or tidy
    his rain;
Yet can I now ask him for the east to get light?
I hang my head, draw in my legs, how narrow and confined!
When suddenly once more, on my head—drrippp!!![43]

After suffering from the cold and wet, we are huddled up awaiting a happy ending in the dawn or, perhaps, some apt philosophical comment about fate from the poet, when our already overstrained nervous system is subjected to the shattering sensation of an ice cold drop of water hitting us squarely on the head!

The perceptive reader will notice a great similarity between Yang Wan-li's drop of ice cold water and the clubbing and shouting of the Lin-chi Ch'an masters or the even more drastic measures of our friend Chü-chih, and it is not surprising that the Southern Sung poet and critic Liu K'o-chuang, who intensely admired Yang Wan-li, wrote:

If we make a comparison with Buddhism, Huang T'ing-chien was the first patriarch. Lü Pen-chung and Tseng Chi [1084–1166] were the Northern and Southern Schools of Ch'an. Yang Wan-li appeared somewhat later like Te-shan [d. 867], founder of the Lin-chi Sect. The first patriarch and those immediately following him only used "words," but when Yang Wan-li's clubbing and shouting appeared, things became considerably more active. . . . Both Hsü Ssu-tao and Hsü Ssu-sun meditated under Yang Wan-li, and their startling lines are frequently similar to his.[44]

Thus, we see that Liu K'o-chuang thought that Huang T'ing-chien, founder of the Kiangsi school, was similar to early Ch'an masters, who were still attached to words and had not yet been enlightened to the basic doctrine of later Ch'an masters "not to set up words," that is, not to become attached to verbal formulations. Yang Wan-li, on the other hand, was similar to the Lin-chi master Te-shan, who either clubbed or shouted at students who remained attached to language and the discursive thought which accompanies it. By means of his "clubbing and shouting," Yang Wan-li did not slip back into the cycle of "transmigration and death," but was able to escape the limitations of language.

V *Humor*

It is hoped that by now the reader has noticed the use of humor in the poems of Yang Wan-li translated above, and, in fact, humor is one of the most important elements of Yang's live method. Of course, it would be futile to ascribe Yang's humor completely to Ch'an Buddhism or the influence of any other school of thought, but we can certainly understand his humor better in the context of the influence Ch'an had on his literary theories and poetic creation.

As we have already noticed, Yang uses the startling to produce the effect of "sudden enlightenment" in his verse. However, much good humorous literature uses the unexpected in very similar manner to elicit humor, and the act of laughter itself, in its suddenness bears a definite affinity to enlightenment. Thus, we find that when we read Ch'an works written during T'ang and Sung times, we are often excited into laughter by their ability to shock us with their irrational humor: "One day P'u-hua was eating raw vegetables in front of the monk's hall. Upon seeing him, the master Yi-hsüan said: 'You look just like a donkey!' P'u-hua immediately brayed like a donkey. The master retorted: 'You bandit!' P'u-hua shouted: 'Bandits! Bandits!' and immediately raced away."[45]

Although very little of Yang Wan-li's early poetry is humorous, since he was still under the influence of the Kiangsi poets, as early as 1168 we can already see a hint of what was to come later:

I Follow Behind Uncle Ch'ang-ying to Go out Visiting on
"Man" Day at Dawn

Each of the four seasons has its good points,
But, in the end, none are like the spring.
What need have we of flowers and willows
To love the splendor of the spring season?
This morning I went out walking
Following behind uncle to the west of South Hill.
The mud is so soft, my sandals are cozy,
The wind so tender, my face doesn't feel it.
Cold grasses begin to move their warm sprouts,
While clear mountains retain the appearance of rain.
Water and sun flirt with one another;
In wrinkled ripples is born a shattered radiance.
How could this bird song be just for my sake?
Yet listening to it, I am by chance delighted.
When I went outdoors I first feared trouble,
But now on the road, I forget to go home.
As long as my mind is satisfied,
What matter if I go out or stay home?
A passerby sees me and bows
Just when I'm thinking of something.
I don't even see his face
And answer with what comes to my mouth.
Only later I awaken and fear I've insulted him;
I want to beg forgiveness, but can't catch up.
Perhaps, my frankness will seem insolent,
But if he's angry, then what can *I* do?[46]

Of course, the humor of this early poem is quite subtle, but in it we see the germs of Yang Wan-li's later writing. In the first part of the poem, Yang shows himself to be totally in harmony with nature. Although he knows his importance to the natural world is negligible, he finds great delight in the mysterious processes whereby nature renews herself in the early spring, and as a result, he is lost in a sort of reverie in which he transcends social conventions. However, unnatural society soon intrudes into Yang's dream world, and when he finally awakens, he is worried by his neglect of the decorum of social life. In the end the natural side of Yang wins, and he concludes, somewhat unsocially, that since there is nothing he can do to correct his mistake, he might as well forget it. The humor of this poem is more difficult for the modern Westerner to fathom, for we are not as easily shocked in social matters as were the medieval Chinese. Yet we can readily recognize an affinity between the humor of Yang's poem and the irreverent attitude of the Sung dynasty Ch'an masters such as Hui-k'ai, author of the *Pass Without a Gate*, who as we have seen, refers to the Buddha as "yellow-faced Gautama."

After Yang's poetic enlightenment his humor was no longer so restrained as in his earlier works, and he fully mastered the use of the unexpected or shocking to make the reader laugh. In 1178, Yang wrote:

On Hearing the Wind's Sound at Night

When he makes it hot or cold, there's nowhere for me
    to escape;
He opens flowers and fells them, suiting his own fancy.
It's his sound at night that's especially despicable,
For he's bent on distracting this sad man's midnight sleep.
Since he is formless, how can he have a voice?
Without reason, the trees help him make noise.
I'm going to cut down all the old catalpas and
    withered willows;
And then we'll just see what the hell he can do about *that!*[47]

In this poem, the poet takes the offensive against the wind and the unexpected violence of the author's assault upon the poor catalpas and willows surprises the reader into laughter. Thus, we may conclude that although much of Yang Wan-li's humorous verse has little to do with Ch'an Buddhism directly, the technique of his humor is similar in its use of surprise and even violence to the humor so often found in Sung dynasty Ch'an texts themselves.

Yang Wan-li's humor was rarely appreciated by post-Sung critics, for many of the more conservative Ming and Ch'ing authors took such joking to be mere buffoonery. Nevertheless, not all later critics were hostile and the editors of the Sung poetry anthology, *Sung-shih ch'ao*, who were so influential in reviving interest in Sung poetry in Ch'ing times, wrote:

Yang Wan-li's natural endowments were like those of Li Po. He discarded all that was inessential and produced his own "mechanism." When those poems of Yang which the ançients said were similar to Li Po's enter the vulgar eyes of moderns, they all seem to be rustic and crude. After I first obtained the selection of Yang's poems published by the Huang-ch'un Bookshop and those poems recorded by Mr. Kao of Tsui-li, I edited and copied them, and everyone who read them laughed heartily. Alas! That which does not make one laugh is not worthy of being Yang Wan-li's poetry.[48]

VI *Colloquial Language*

In our discussion of Yang Wan-li's theory of poetry, we have already stated that he strongly advocated a simple, unadorned form of verse relatively free from erudite allusions. Yang's attempt to write such natural poetry caused him to regard poetry written in a highly colloquial style to be one of the most important elements of his live method. No scholar poet before him used the colloquial so extensively, and possibly it is significant that the language of his verse displays a marked resemblance to the colloquial of contemporary Ch'an writers, who like Yang did not place so much emphasis on polished refinement. However, we need not necessarily look to the Ch'an monks to find the source for Yang's use of the spoken tongue, for throughout his life, Yang was a great admirer of Po Chü-yi, the poet who was most instrumental in introducing the colloquial language into T'ang dynasty verse:

On the Fifth of the Fifth Month I Stop Drinking Due to Illness

In my sickness I'm so bored I give up sweeping and cleaning;
Not drinking during the holidays makes me even sadder.
By chance I read the *Works of Po Chü-yi;*
Not only has my sadness gone, but my sickness has left, too![49]

It is futile to cite examples of Yang's colloquial verse in translation, for one can only appreciate his dexterous use of the spoken language by reading his poems in the original Chinese. However, throughout this work an attempt has been made to translate Yang's poems into a language as close as possible to spoken English in order to reproduce his colloquial and sometimes even slangy style. Yet, it is nearly impossible to duplicate the effect that Yang's poetry has upon the Chinese reader, for although colloquial phrases abound in his works, his poems are still written in classical Chinese. Yang's love of the spoken language in a literary tradition noted for its obscurity is highly laudable, but the pitfalls of his method are easily apparent. Since the colloquial language tends to be considerably more diffuse than classical Chinese, there is always the danger that the use of too much colloquial, and especially spoken particles such as *liao* and *ma*, will destroy the very compactness which is one of the chief glories of the Chinese poetic tradition. Yang Wan-li himself was fully aware of the problems involved, and, according to his contemporary Lo Ta-ching (ca. 1224), Yang stressed the care with which one should use colloquial language in classical poetry:

Yang Wan-li said: "Certainly there are poems which turn the vulgar into the refined, but this practice must pass through the 'smelting and transformation' of previous generations before it is acceptable. Li Po's use of the colloquial particles *nai-k'o*, Tu Fu's *che-mo*, and the use of *li-hsü* or *jo-ke* of the late T'ang poets are of this category. In their Cold Food Festival poems, the T'ang poets did not dare use the word *t'ang* [colloquial for a type of sweet cake eaten on this festival], and in their Double Nine Festival poems, they did not dare use the word *kao* ['cake']. Wang An-shih did not dare write poems about plum flowers; he did not lightly dare to lead a village woman or peasant man to sit at the side of King P'ing's son and Marquis Wei's wife [in other words, use colloquial language in classical poems]. I have observed that among Tu Fu's poetry there are entire poems which use ordinary and vulgar language without any harm to their superiority or subtlety. [Yang then quotes several examples.]" Yang Wan-li frequently emulated this style, which is so satisfying and delightful.[50]

Although Yang recognizes the dangers of using the spoken language in classical poetry and the necessity for constant refinement of the practice, he makes a strong case for bringing the language of the common man into the poetry of the intellectual elite. As might be expected, many later critics did not agree with Yang's attempts to write artless, colloquial poetry. Typical of these is the Ch'ing poet and critic Chu Yi-tsun (1629–1709): "At present, those who speak of poetry always despise or ignore the sound of the T'ang and enter into the currents and schools of the Sung. The highest take Su Shih and Huang T'ing-chien as their masters, while the lowest imitate the style of Yang Wan-li. They think shouting and clamor to be marvelous and rusticity and crudeness to be correct."[51] Further: "Recently, poets have all abandoned T'ang and imitated Sung. I suspect that Lu Yu was too 'cooked' and Huang T'ing-chien too 'raw.' The raw flowed and became Hsiao Te-tsao [fl. 1160], while the cooked sank and became Yang Wan-li. What difference is there between those who imitate him and one who searches for filth by the side of the sea?"[52] Chu Yi-tsun was attached to the "dead method" of imitation of the ancients, while Yang Wan-li meditated on the liveliness of the spoken language.

CHAPTER 4

Illusion and Reality

W E have already seen how Yang Wan-li uses the Ch'an concept of enlightenment as the central theme in his theory of literature, and as one would expect, Yang's interest in Buddhism had a great influence on the subject matter of much of his poetry. One of the basic problems that occupied the Buddhists was the concept of reality versus illusion, and in line with the Buddhist theory of non-dualism, enlightenment lay in the realization of the identity of reality and illusion. Yang explores this question in one of his late poems (1201):

> Playing with the Moon on a Summer Night
>
> When I raise my head, the moon's in the sky,
> But when it shines on me, my shadow's on the ground.
> As I walk, my shadow walks, too;
> When I stop, my shadow also stops.
> I wonder if my shadow and I
> Are one thing or maybe two.
> The moon can trace out my shadow,
> But if it traced its own, I wonder what it'd be like.
> By chance, I pace by the bank of a stream,
> And now, the moon is in the stream!
> Above and below, altogether two moons;
> Which of them is the real one?
> Or is the water the sky?
> Or the sky the water?[1]

The reflection of the moon in the water as a symbol of reality versus illusion is not originally Chinese and is already found in the *prajñā*, or wisdom, literature, which shook Chinese thought when it was introduced at the end of the third century. In describing the charac-

78

teristics of a *bodhisattva*, or supreme enlightened being, the *Pañcaviṁśati-sāhāsrikā-prajñā-pāramitā-sūtra*, translated into Chinese by Kumārajīva (344–414), states that the enlightened being "understands all *dharmas* to be like a sleight of hand, a mirage, the moon in the water, the void, an echo, a *gandharva* city [mirage], a dream, a shadow, the reflection in a mirror, or a transformation."[2] The commentary in the famed Buddhist work *Ta-chih-tu lun* on this passage reads:

As for its being like the moon in the water, the moon is really in the sky, but its reflection appears in the water. The moon, like the mark of the real *dharma*, is as if in the "sky" of the reality of the true *dharma* nature. In the "water" of the mind of all gods and men there appear the marks of the ego and all that belongs to the ego, and for this reason it is said to be like the moon in the water. Moreover, if a small child sees the moon in the water, he is glad and wishes to grab it, but when an adult sees this, he laughs.[3]

In other words, all phenomenal existence, which consists of *dharmas*, is no more real than the reflection of the moon in water, and those who are enlightened realize the falsity of such external appearances.

As early as the Liang dynasty (502–557), the ten metaphors for illusion from the *prajñā* literature served as poetic material, and the Buddhist emperors of the Liang dynasty, Wu Ti (*reg.* 502–550) and Chien-wen Ti (*reg.* 550–551) both wrote poems on each of these metaphors. In his poem "Water Moon" Chien-wen Ti writes:

> A round wheel, it shines on the water;
> New born, it also reflects on the current.
> Full, full, like a soaked jade ring;
> Clear, clear, like a sunken hook.
> Though not worried about its hare drowning,
> How can its cassia-tree branches float?
> Although it vainly causes people to appreciate this,
> It may still serve to delight a jumping monkey.
> A myriad troubles seem dissolved, washed away;
> What further marks are there to search for?[4]

Thus, by the time Yang wrote about the reflection of the moon in the water, it was already widely known as a metaphor for the illusion of the world. Nevertheless, Yang certainly was the first poet to

substitute wine for water, the result of which was probably his finest
philosophical poem:

> Two Days After Double Nine I Climb with Hsü K'e-chang
> to Myriad Flowers River Valley and Pass the Wine
> Cup Beneath the Moon

This old fellow's really thirsty, but the moon's
    thirstier still;
As soon as the wine falls into my cup, the moon's
    already inside.
She brings in the blue sky along with her,
So both moon and sky are soaking wet.
"The sky loves wine" has been handed down from ancient times,
But "the moon doesn't know how to drink" is really
    reckless talk.
I raise my cup and swallow the moon down with one gulp,
Yet when I raise my head I see the moon still in the sky.
This old fellow laughs and asks his guest,
"Is there just one moon or are there two?"
The wine enters my poet's intestines—wind and fire
    burst out;
The moon enters my poet's intestines—ice and snow
    pour forth.
Before I can down one cup, my poem is already finished;
I recite the poem to heaven and even heaven is startled.
How do I know that the myriad ages are just some dried-
    up bones?
I pour out some wine and gulp down another moon![5]

Yang obviously regarded this poem as one of his most important
creations, for the poet Lo Ta-ching, who was a friend of Yang's
eldest son and from the same village as the Yang family, wrote:

Yang Wan-li's poem about passing the wine cup under the moon is as
follows [poem quoted]. When I was about ten years old, I waited on my
father, the Old Man of Bamboo Valley, while we visited Yang Wan-li, and I
heard Yang recite this poem with my own ears, after which he said: "I will
say myself that this work of mine is similar to Li Po's!"[6]

The style of the poem is certainly influenced by Li Po, but the wine
drinking in Yang's poem is Buddhist compared to the Taoist content
of Li's works. The moon in the wine corresponds to the same moon

in the creek water in our first poem, with the same mixture of reality and illusion. Through the elixir of Chinese poetry, namely wine, an Indian philosophical concept is expressed in a uniquely Chinese way.

When one reads the list of the ten metaphors for illusion from the *prajñā* literature, one notices that a number of them, such as the "mirage" or "echo," are not only illusory in appearance or sound but also of extremely short duration. Yang Wan-li had a particular interest in phenomena of short duration, and although he is not entirely alone in this interest among Sung poets, he was probably the most successful in describing such objects. Indeed, it is not improbable that he had the "mirage" of the *prajñā* literature in mind when he described what happens when one looks at a lamp early in the morning before one has totally awakened to the realm of ordinary consciousness:

Getting Up Early on an Autumn Day

> The cock's crowed but the bell hasn't rung yet,
> So I don't know if it's dawn or not.
> I get up, but I'm afraid I'll waken everybody,
> And I don't dare open the windows.
> The leftover lamp spits forth its pointed horn rays;
> Above and below it, two silver broomsticks form.
> I focus my eyes, trying to examine them closely,
> But they scatter, racing away like a flash of lightning![7]

Yang's interest in phenomena of short duration enabled him to find beauty in occurrences which most earlier poets would not have even noticed. One winter night he left some newly picked plum branches in two vases filled with water. When the water froze and the vases broke, the flowering branches were still stuck in two vase-shaped pieces of ice which Yang Wan-li's poetic genius transformed into crystal vases sent from heaven:

> Who has sent me these two crystal vases,
> With several branches of plum growing in them?
> Their slender branches still bear scars from picking;
> Through the vases I see them reflected, clear to their
> bones.
> The big branches have opened completely, flowers
> like snow;

The small branches, not yet opened, are purer by far.
They vie in bursting forth from the vases' mouths;
Alas! One can only look and not pick!

They say that when crystal has just appeared in
    the myriad chasms,
About to harden, not yet hard, it's like frozen lard.
Above, there was a river plum, its flowers at their peak;
Several branches were blown off and fell on these
    cold crystal mirrors.
A jade carver cut them out and brought them to this world,
Polishing out these vases with the plums for us to see.
Even now there are places where they haven't hardened,
And in the vases, pearls of water race back and forth.
All that worries me is the spring sun reddening outside
    my window,
For it will soon turn my vases into "Mister No-suches."[8]

Through the medium of Yang's poetic fancy, two pieces of ice are
magically changed into crystal vases sent by some mysterious jade
carver from the land of the immortals. The only problem with the
fantasy Yang has created is that in a few hours it will have melted
away into nothing.

For Yang Wan-li, the ordinary world of "common sense" is full of
mysterious optical illusions. When he watches the sun setting over a
lake, it seems to enter directly into the water:

I sit and watch the west sun set over the lake shore;
It's not swallowed by mountains, nor are there any clouds.
Inch by inch, it comes lower and suddenly sinks completely;
Clearly it's entered the water, but there aren't any
    traces left behind![9]

Or when Yang observes a fisherman floating away from him on a
small boat, the fisherman in his grass raincoat seems to turn into a
goose perched on a reed:

The fisherman and his boat enter the tortuous lake,
And my old eyes are very diligent in watching him.
I look back and forth, but something strange happens;
He changes into a lone goose perched on a horizontal
    reed![10]

In China and India, one of the most common symbols for the illusion and brevity of life is the bubble:

Bubbles

A pale sun, light clouds, the rain drops are sparse;
Water bubbles follow the rain, arising in the pure ditch.
Jumping here, racing there, as on a jasper platter,
They create dragon palace pearls an inch in diameter.

The bubbles seem to be dragon palace pearls, but in a second, they have burst and are no more:

How can we ever get to know the greatest treasures
completely?
These black dragon pearls float, then disappear in
an instant.
Just as the ornament on the forehead of the Golden Immortal,
They only let ordinary folk see one half of themselves.[11]

The "Golden Immortal" is the Buddha and the ornament on his forehead is the pearl sunk into the forehead of a Buddhist statue to represent the Buddha's divine eye. Of course, only one half is visible to the observer just as one sees only one half of the "sphere" of a bubble. Thus, the bubble not only becomes a symbol of the brevity of temporal existence but also, somewhat ironically, a symbol for the secrets of the universe, denied to the ordinary eye and reserved only for the enlightened. By making the ephemeral into a symbol for the eternal, Yang comes close to transcending the dualism between illusion and reality.

CHAPTER 5

The World of Man

I Family and Children

YANG Wan-li's interest in mundane affairs was partially a result of his Ch'an inspired view of literature, but as a Confucian scholar official, he was obliged to occupy himself with the affairs of the world of man. The focal point of daily life for the Chinese intellectual from the most ancient times was the Chinese extended family. The scholar's career in government was largely an expression of the family's desire for increasing its wealth and prestige, and although the Sung examination system held out great rewards for the ambitious individual, the family always benefitted from the accomplishments of its members. However, in spite of this overriding importance of the family system, it is quite strange that not until the eighth century do we find much mention of the family in classical poetry. T'ao Ch'ien's "Poem of Scolding his Sons"[1] is a notable exception to this rule, but Tu Fu was really the first poet to write about his wife and children to any extent, and such a poem as "The Moonlit Night" is very innovative in the highly personal description of the relation between the poet and his wife.[2] Tu Fu is one of the most important figures in the overthrow of the aristocratic conventions of literature, which had been formed during the North-south Period, and, hence, he was able to write about a subject which was considered undignified by earlier writers of a more "refined" age.

By Northern Sung times the aristocrats and their literary pretensions had disappeared, so that Sung authors felt free to deal with subject matter that would have horrified an aristocratic poet. Therefore, the Sung poets wrote about their parents, children, wives, and even concubines to a much greater degree than ever before. The following work by Yang Wan-li is typical of the new spirit present in Sung verse:

When my term as Governor of Ling-ling has finished but no replacement comes, my father takes our old and young back home first. As I send them out of the city, we meet up with rain and mud, so a myriad emotions suddenly gather in me.

> My father went home first, but I can't go yet;
> My mother's already set off, but she still looks back at me.
> The children are happy to go home; they don't understand
>   sorrow yet;[3]
> I'm sad, for how could I be foolish as a child?
> People watching from the city wall shouldn't feel envy,
> For how can a settled man understand a wanderer's woes?
> Luckily, yesterday was clear, but today there's rain again;
> When did the Lord of Heaven ever worry about travelers'
>   hardships?
> My mother's lungs are ailing, and she greatly fears the cold,
> So the evening wind hasn't cause to moan through my room.
> People all raise their sons to become officials,
> But *who* was it that caused father's trip to be like this?[4]

Yang concurs with what we have said about pressure from the family being the main force propelling men into official careers, but Yang also suggests a tension between his filial piety toward his parents and his official duties, for his absence from home is the main cause of his parents' discomfort.

We have frequently noticed a strong contradiction between personal ethical standards and public official duties in Yang's government career, but it is very informative to find the same dichotomy existing in his family life. Although pre-Sung Confucian society had idealized the stern, autocratic father, Yang Wan-li and other Sung authors treated their sons as friends:

I receive a letter from my two sons Shou-jen and Shou-chün stating they were unable to take their examinations because of illness and informing me of the date of their arrival.

> When will my two sons arrive?
> The three autumn months are nearly ended.
> Receiving your half piece of paper
> Washed away a year of my sadness.
> I lack strength in my fur chisel writing brush;

No reason for my ink to be ashamed.
The sea and mountains are colder and more azure;
I arrange my carriage to await your companionship.[5]

This spirit of friendship on equal terms became particularly strong in the poems that Yang wrote after his retirement:

When Tz'u-kung's period of service is completed, he returns home. By chance, the *Shang-ssu* and Cold Food Festivals are on the same day, so father and son have a small drink together.

Once again it's the time of year for purification rituals,
But what need have *we* for floating metal cups in the
    twisting stream?[6]
Tasting all the different kinds of wine, I'm drunk with
    just a little;
I sit until the third watch, when it's still not too late
    to sleep.
By chance, *Shang-ssu* is on the Day of Cold Food,
Yet the spring wind is too stingy to let peonies bloom.
White-haired father and son talk in front of the lamp,
Forgetting their long parting midst the rivers and lakes.[7]

Although the more informal family relations reflected in Yang's poetry were being written about by such poets as Mei Yao-ch'en over a hundred years before Yang's time, Yang's attitude toward children is very original.[8] Tu Fu wrote about his children with great affection, and even such a refined poet as Li Shang-yin wrote a poem "Bragging about my Son."[9] However, Yang was the first poet who attempted to enter into the child's own world, an interest which was also shared by Southern Sung painters, who painted a number of works on the following theme:

Watching a Children's Festival for Welcoming a God

Their flower caps are about an ounce heavy,
And their silk robes shine like autumn water.
They try hard to walk but end up dawdling;
Attempting to sing elegantly, they just get bashful.
A parrot perches on one of their leeklike fingers,[10]
While lotuses load a brocade float.
Don't watch the little children's festival,
For it only makes an old man sadder.[11]

Adults do not enter into Yang's description of the children's festival in the same way that they are usually excluded from contemporary paintings of children's celebrations. Only in the last two lines of the poem does the adult world intrude, and such nostalgia for lost youth is certainly one of the reasons behind the Southern Sung interest in children as literary and artistic subjects, for the loss of youth is a symbol for worldly corruption. In his "Poems on Returning to the Fields," T'ao Ch'ien, the father of Chinese nature verse, states that he was originally free from corruption during his youth, but he became tainted by the dust of the world only after entering official life.[12] Centuries before T'ao, the *Tao-te ching* had compared the perfect man to a baby,[13] and on the Confucian side, Mencius' doctrine of man's originally good nature suggests the purity of children compared to adults.

Yang Wan-li felt that children live in their own realm of "reality" quite apart from the humdrum existence of the adult:

Garden of Youth

When we were residing at Rush Bridge, there was a square rock in the garden which someone dug out and filled with soil. My little grandson planted flowers and vegetables in it, and in jest I named it "Garden of Youth."

> Our residence's backyard is hardly half a pace long;
> His garden is made from swallow's mud, the wall from pebbles.
> One or two plants of lucky incense and day lily;[14]
> Three or four clumps of leek leaves and nasturtium sprouts.
> The little boy opens up his small Gold Valley Villa,[15]
> And a snail chooses the site to build another pearl palace.
> I wish I could go every day and play with the boy there,
> But I think only an ant could make it through the path![16]

In adult terms the child's garden is totally illusory, but for the child it has a reality which is as valid as the "reality" of adult life. Yang wishes that he could escape from the adult world of official responsibilities, but the gulf between adult and child cannot be bridged. In addition to the Confucian and Taoist elements in the poem, the work can be interpreted with Ch'an concepts also. To Yang, the child's world symbolizes a state in which such "rational" concepts as space and time are eliminated and one is free of the discursive thought which impedes casting off the realm of dust. The sixteenth-century "wildcat Ch'an" thinker Li Chih (1529–1602) similarly insists that one must return to his "child mind" in order to gain freedom from the trammels of mundane existence.[17] Although Li Chih was also deeply influenced by Taoist thought, such an idea is similar to the Mahāyānist Buddhist contention that an originally pure Buddha Nature (fo-hsing) exists in all things, and it only becomes defiled through desire and thought.

Such an idea of original purity from such emotions as sadness is hinted at in the second line of a short poem Yang wrote while on a boat voyage:

I Make Fun of a Little Boy

On a boat in the rain, we feel so cooped up;
Even a little boy *without* sadness becomes sad.
I've watched you sit there sleeping, not once were you awake;
But when I tell you to go to bed, you just wag your head![18]

Although the poem lacks any of the philosophical pretensions of some of Yang's other verse on children, once again we observe Yang's subtle understanding of a child's psychology, and the gentle humor of the poem corresponds to what we find in Yang's other poetry about his family. In general, Yang Wan-li's poetry on the family displays the same interest in everyday life and consciousness of the seeming contradiction between the mundane and the absolute that we find in all of his works.

II *The Scholar Poet's Place in Society*

In addition to describing his relationship with his family, Yang's poetry frequently deals with the scholar-official's day-to-day life. When the official was not occupied with his paperwork, he spent much of his time reading books, and Yang's attitude toward the activity of book learning is closely related to his theories of poetic creation that we have already discussed. Book learning probably occupied a higher position in China than in any other culture, and the worship of the written word was nothing new in Sung times. Yang himself felt that there was no diversion more enjoyable than reading a book in the cold winter season:

Gazing from Lichee Hall During the Evening
(Second Poem of Three)

My sickly bones, emaciated by autumn, fear the evening, pure;
A cool wind stealthily brings the north wind, light.
To repel the cold the window frames are pasted over double;[19]
Only letting in a few eyes of light next to my book.[20]

The widespread use of printing during the Sung dynasty allowed the Chinese to read even more than they had in T'ang times, and the cult of the bibliophile became increasingly popular. Now the Chinese scholar became deeply involved in acquiring a huge collection of books, paying large sums of money for high quality printing and rare editions. Yang himself collected some rare books during his youth and fully appreciated the differences between good and bad editions:

I Thank the Tea Secretary of Chien-chou, Wu Te-hua, for
Sending Me a New Edition of Su Shih's Works

Yellow gold, white jade-rings, bright moon pearls,
Pure song, wonderful dances, and beauties who topple cities,
Other houses have them but my house doesn't;
Like Ssu-ma Hsiang-ju, all *I* have are four walls around me.[21]
Beside them, I have a shelf of books,
But they can't fill me up, they just fill the bookworms.
An old friend sends Su Shih's works from afar,
And my old books leave their seats to make way for them.
While a boy, I was never lazy about playing around,
But when anyone talked of reading, I got up late on purpose.
My Dad got mad and scolded me for being such a lout,
So I forced my hungry intestines to devour worm-eaten pages.
As I got older, all my business fell behind others,
And I casually used old books to screen my sick eyes.[22]
When my sick eyes met a book, they suddenly went fuzzy;
Under my writing brush, fly-head characters turned to old ravens.[23]
With such bad eyes, what could I do with old books?
For as soon as I opened one, I could merely sigh.
Although I already have the writings of Su Shih,
Before I can finish the last chapter, my hand already quits.
The printer's ink is blurred, and the paper bad;
It has neither fishnet paper nor tadpole-head writing.[24]

The *new* book's words, freshly carved on Fu-sha datewood,
Were copied then cut, sparse and lean, just like an original.[25]
The paper is like snow cocoons from a jade bowl;
While the characters are frosty geese dotting the autumn clouds.
As I get older, both of my eyes seem lost in a fog;
Coming across willows or flowers, I don't even glance.[26]
Only if I meet with books, excellent and new,
Do I play with them all day; how could I leave them?
Su Shih was even wilder than I am;
He wouldn't exchange his serge for the three noblest posts.
He hanged the tip of his writing brush on the moon's ribs;[27]
And the common horses of all ages were hardly worth deflating.[28]
My old friend pities me, old and ever clumsier,
But he doesn't send a golden pill to prop up my sick bones.[29]
No, *he* sends this book along to vex me;
Snuffing out the drab lamp, I scratch my white hair.[30]

In line with the bibliophile tradition, Yang praises the quality of
paper and clarity of print, but in the last few lines of the poem it
becomes apparent he is making fun of the same tradition, when he
suggests his friend would have been more considerate to send some
medicine rather than a costly edition of Su Shih's poems.

However, Yang is attacking the bookish attitude of the Sung
scholar even before the conclusion of the poem, for he states that
excessive study was contrary to his natural inclinations as a child,
and we have already seen how Yang considered children to be purer
than adults. Yang hints strongly at the philosophical background to
his ridicule of the bibliophile when he alludes to using books as a
screen for his eyes, an idea originating in the Ch'an work *Ching-te
ch'uan-teng lu*. Just as the Ch'an masters felt *sūtras* were only of use
for shading the eyes, Yang suggests that the *"sūtras"* of the classical
poets, the "great" works of the past, were equally useless to one who
truly wanted to obtain complete poetic enlightenment.

Yang describes the futility of scholarly activities in a poem he
wrote much earlier in his life, when he had just begun to reject Sung
bookishness:

In Answer to Chung-liang's Extemporaneous Poem on the End of Spring
(Fourth Poem of Five)

When poor, it's hard to invite Uncle Wine over;[31]
Sick, how could I ride a copper-string piebald?

Even in my dreams, can I go to see the flowers?
For spring suddenly disappears midst the rain.
Plow-deep rain makes for a harvest of five pecks;
A hundred silkworm racks await the third sleep.[32]
Only the scholar of books is foolish,
For all year long he plows on paper fields.[33]

The poverty and sickliness of the scholar contrast vividly with the creative activities of rice planting and sericulture, for the peasant at least plows real fields, but the scholar reaps no worthwhile harvests.

The ornate, allusive style of Yang's poem proves he was still under the influence of the *"sūtras"* of his Kiangsi masters, and it was not until after his enlightenment that he could reject the Sung cult of the book in its entirety:

Don't Read Books

Don't read books!
Don't chant poetry!
If you read books, your eyes become so withered you
can see the bones.
If you chant poetry, each word must be vomited from
your heart.
People say reading books is a joy;
They say chanting poems is good.
Your lips always buzz like an autumn bug,
And you only get scrawny and old!
If you get scrawny and old it's of little account,
But when people hear you, they get annoyed.
It's better to close your eyes and sit in your study,
Lower the curtains, sweep the floor, and burn incense
by yourself.
There's a flavor in listening to the wind and the rain;
When you're strong, walk, when you're tired, sleep![34]

Yang had experienced his sudden enlightenment only a few months before he wrote this poem, and now he had taken leave of all his old masters and set out in a new direction.

Yang's attitude toward the principal activity of the scholar-official suggests a strong alienation toward the entire range of activities in which the scholar-official was supposed to engage. We have already

noticed this revulsion Yang felt toward the official career that occupied most of his life, but the poet felt an even more fundamental
alienation toward the whole of society. Yang was by no means alone
in this feeling, for his friend Chu Hsi (1130–1200) voiced similar
sentiments, and, in fact, Yang's attitude was extremely prevalent in
earlier times in China. Yang gave vent to his frustration in a despair-
ing poem written during a return to his native village:

Returning Home Drunk the Next Day

As the day gets late, I really want to go home,
But my host takes pains to make me stay.
It's not that I'm unable to drink;
Old and sick, I fear the cups and counters.[35]
We cannot offend other people's feelings,
Though I want to go, I end up tarrying.
I'm drunk, so he finally gives in,
Drunk, but why should I worry about that?
On the road home, my mind is drowsy, drowsy;
The setting sun lies on the mountain range's tip.
Somebody's house sits in the bamboos;
I want to rest, so I drop in for a spell.
An old man is delighted that I've come
And addresses me "prince, lord."
I tell him: "I'm no such thing,"
But he bows and smiles, just shaking his head.
My worldly schemes disappeared long ago,
But there still are seagulls that won't come down.[36]
Even this old peasant is alienated from me;
I'm old, with whom can I play?[37]

Yang feels greatly restricted by his knowledge that while living in
human society "we cannot offend other people's feelings." However, although in his drunkenness Yang seems to momentarily
transcend worldly matters, he is eventually thwarted by the alienation between himself and the peasant, caused by the class differences inherent in societies. Yang realizes that his freedom from
"worldly schemes" cuts him off from ordinary social intercourse, yet
he must still live in the world of men.

As a poet, Yang felt that he was particularly out of joint with his
own society, for the cares of government service continually dis-
rupted the creative impulses of the writer:

On the Third Day of the First Month I Spend the Night
at the Fan Clan Village
(Second Poem of Four)

Tramping around outdoors, I think of a subtle poem,
And I don't spit it out right away but savor it awhile.
The fleet-footed messenger suddenly gives a shout,
A letter has arrived from afar.
I open the seal; just some trite talk of the weather;
Besides this, no further matter.
My wonderful feelings have already vanished;
As I try to recall, I can't remember them.
I was so happy, but suddenly I'm depressed;
Vulgar things truly ruin ones thoughts.
A mountain magpie lands in the empty garden,
And he converses with me, brimming over with joy.
With a laugh, I get up and dust off my clothes;
After all, *my* mind is free of impediments![38]

The "trite talk" which comes from the external world interrupts the process of creativity, an experience which Yang must have suffered continuously in the exhausting position of a public servant. Nonetheless, the poem suggests the path to resolving the contradiction between the creative and worldly life, for Yang is freed of his distress as soon as he realizes that his inner purity protects him from the corrupting influences of the outside world.

Despite the possibility of transcending the world, the lot of the *literatus* poet is far from happy, and his almost certain poverty is one of the most disturbing aspects of his life:

Written in Jest
(First Poem of Two)

The wild chrysanthemum and barren moss each coins money;[39]
With golden yellow and copper green they compete in elegance.
The Lord of Heaven pays these to the impoverished poet,
But they only buy pure sorrow, not any fields![40]

The poet may be poor, but the immortality of a Li Po cannot be measured in monetary terms:

Gazing at Li Po's Grave on the Hsieh Family's Green Mountain
(First Poem of Two)

Hsieh T'iao had a whole village to himself on Green Mountain,[41]
And people of the region summoned his soul year after year.[42]
Where are all those imperial tombs of the Six Dynasties?
Only the grave of the Immortal of Poetry remains beneath the moon.[43]

Compared to the Immortal of Poetry, Li Po, the aristocrats and
royalty of past ages count for nothing. By the time Yang reached old
age, he already had realized that he would be among the immortals
of Chinese literature, and he was conscious of his place in an undy-
ing stream of creativity where there is neither past nor present:

Chanting While Drunk

The ancients are gone, the ancients remain;
If they don't remain, then Heaven should change.
Without leaving behind their three and five line poems,
How could they have earned the love of millions of men?
You men of today laugh at the ancients for being crazy,
But the ancients laugh at you; don't you know?
Morning comes, evening goes, how long will it last for us?
Leaves fall and flowers bloom, never an end to that.
Ordinary people only seek official seals as big as a ladle[44]
Never worrying about the metal club bashing in their mouths.[45]
When alive, all they know is wrinkling their brows;
Dead, where can they ever get another cup of wine?
Oh! Li Po! Oh! Juan Chi![46]
In your days who didn't laugh at you two old men?
The wise and foolish of the past are now all white bones,
But you two old men are a pure wind between heaven and earth![47]

Yang indulges in the poet's vanity that the poet's life is more mean-
ingful and less subject to mortality than ordinary men who "seek
official seals," for the poets of the past live on in the hearts of present
and future men.

Yang's view that the poet endured forever was nothing new in
China, but he went one step further than earlier writers and even
denied the importance of posterity to the creative poet:

On Leaving the River Mouth at Cross Mountain

A white jade badge mountain right by the river shore;
A green flag—it must be an inn.[48]

Jagged cliffs encroach on the house, narrow;
A slender path enters the door, slanting.
The county seat is near, for I see a pair of pagodas;
An island lies horizontal, cut off by a stretch of sand.
Why do I need to wait for strangers coming after me
Before I can believe that this poem is good?[49]

In this work Yang is mocking the modern reader in the same fashion he felt Li Po and Juan Chi were mocking himself and his contemporaries. The underlying belief in the transcendant nature of the poet's vocation has a long tradition before it in China, but Yang's rejection of Chinese bookishness put him in a new relationship with his contemporaries and posterity, for now the writing of poetry became a totally personal act. Yang obviously was aware that men of later ages would read his works, but for the most part, he was writing entirely for himself.

III *Social Criticism and Peasant Life*

In his study of Sung poetry, the contemporary Japanese scholar, Yoshikawa Kōjirō, has proposed the theory that one of the most distinctive characteristics of Sung poetry is the deep sense of social commitment possessed by most of the poets, and Yang Wan-li was certainly no exception to Yoshikawa's idea, as can be seen from his defense of the common people throughout his official career.[50] However, one could easily object to Yoshikawa that many of the most famous T'ang poets were equally involved with the lower classes, and to a large degree such an objection is perfectly valid. Nevertheless, although Yoshikawa does not explore this problem very thoroughly in his book, he is quite correct in maintaining that the attitudes of T'ang and Sung authors toward the peasants differed fundamentally.

Such T'ang poets as Tu Fu and Po Chü-yi, who criticized oppression of the peasantry, were working in a tradition that ultimately dates back to Han and even Chou times. According to Han commentators on the Chou dynasty *Classic of Poetry*, the folk songs of that work were gathered together by royal officers to determine the feelings of the people toward the government,[51] and we supposedly owe the preservation of Han and later folk *yüeh-fu*, or "music bureau" poems, to a continuation of the same practice.[52] It is, thus, no coincidence that Po Chü-yi called his poems of social protest "New Music Bureau Poems," for he subscribed to the view that his descriptions of the peasant should serve as a warning to the govern-

ment to correct abuses and forestall political upheaval.[53] The greater compassion which Tu Fu and Po Chü-yi felt for the peasant was a
symptom of a genuine widening of the concept of humanity, or *jen*,
among T'ang intellectuals, yet one should not forget that T'ang writers were largely interested in the peasant as a political barometer
which would warn of impending storms in the countryside. As long
as the peasant was reasonably well fed and did not complain too
loudly, the T'ang intellectual was satisfied to direct his attention to
other subjects. To such men as Tu Fu and Po Chü-yi the peasant
existed largely as an abstraction, which was a convenient vehicle for
voicing criticism against a corrupt and inept government.

In Sung times the peasant could serve the same purpose, and
much of Yang's peasant poetry is written in a vein similar to the
T'ang masters:

> Passing White Sand, a Bamboo Branch Song[54]
> (Third Poem of Six)

> How I love these two or three homes in the mountain depths;
> They don't plant fragrant rice but only hemp.
> After they plow all along the dike, they hoe the whole mountain,
> But what kind of living can they get from all this?[55]

Yang is specifically concerned with the acute land shortage which
plagued China in Southern Sung times as a result of the huge
number of refugees who escaped south and the unprecedented
growth of the local population.

Yang's poem is certainly a very effective criticism of the land
shortage, but there is an unusual element in the work which makes
it stand out from more one-dimensional social criticism found in Po
Chü-yi's poetry.[56] Yang's pity for the peasants seems to grow out of a
much more intimate contact with peasant life than T'ang intellectuals possessed, for Yang was fully acquainted with the austere setting
in which the Chinese peasant attempted to eke out a livelihood.
This firsthand experience of rural life evokes an intense admiration
in Yang for the industrious farmers who even plow the mountains.
Yang does not just see the poor peasant as an abstract symbol for the
inability of the government to resolve the land problem, but he
truly respects the farmer because of his herculean labors in keeping
alive.

Another poem in which Yang shows his sympathies for the lower classes allows us to form a clearer picture of how his peasant poetry differed from earlier works:

The Boat People[57]

> The Lord of Heaven has ordained him a life on water;
> From youth he is taught to tread the wave flowers.
> He boils crabs for food, so how could he know rice?
> Twists banana fibers for cloth, what need of gauze?
> Last night the spring flood swallowed a sand bank,
> So he hurriedly sends his son to cut some reed sprouts.[58]
> I laugh at myself for being on the road all my life,
> But *he* floats his *house* about midst piles of silver waves.[59]

Yang's choice of subject matter is quite extraordinary, for he does not describe the plight of the ordinary land peasant but writes of the Tanka minority instead. To earlier T'ang poets such as Li Po the life of the boat people was highly romantic, for their watery existence seemed to set them apart from the normal world of everyday existence.[60] Yang rejects this romanticized view of the boat people and depicts the actual conditions under which they lived. He attacks the imperial court's unfair policy toward the boat people when he says the "Lord of Heaven," that is, the emperor, condemns them to their wretched fate, but his work is more realistic than the typical Po Chü-yi protest poem, for Yang's boatman goes about his everyday activities in spite of his miserable existence. This realism of Yang's poem as opposed to earlier protest verse shows that he was no longer interested in the lower classes as an abstract symbol for the inequalities of society, but that he is willing to view the common people as human beings on the same level as himself.

In addition to using the peasant as a political barometer, the Chinese intellectual wrote about peasants, because by the fall of the Han dynasty they had become a symbol for the escape from the boring routine and personal hazards of the official career. Thus, T'ao Ch'ien retired to a peasantlike existence because he could not bear to "bend his waist for five pecks of rice."[61] Yang himself sometimes had similar feelings:

In Late Spring I Walk in the Fields at South Flats

> In the west field day before yesterday, dust had turned
> to clouds;

But in the south village today, waves form on the road.[62]
Cloudy rice has always stayed distant from us Kuang-wen scholars,[63]
Yet why should I refuse braving rain to learn farming?
The peasants say: "Our rice seedlings are better than
   the wheat,
But they're still like green needles and unfit to eat."[64]
All my life I've never stuck my fingers in the mud;
How can my fur-chisel writing brush be haughty to
   peasant raincoats?
I just hope our frontiers won't have any more problems,
For my only ambition in life is to cultivate wheat
   clouds with a hoe.
I won't worry if my official horse is sent back to the
   government,
Because if I borrow an ox to ride home, I won't even
   need a saddle![65]

Yang's poem is different from the typical pre-Sung work, which contrasts the idyllic surroundings of rural life with the tension and anxieties of an official career; for despite Yang's yearning for the simplicity of country living, he expresses his guilt feelings toward the laboring masses who supported the whole intricate bureaucracy through their taxes. Such sentiments had already been voiced by Po Chü-yi in the ninth century,[66] but Yang's poem is distinguished again by a much greater realism; although he claims he has never stuck his fingers in the mud, his intimate knowledge of the conditions of the rice harvest proves he had lived in close contact with the peasants. The older romantic view of the peasant as some sort of otherworldly creature had been altered by a closer acquaintance with the grim facts of peasant existence.

The greater realism with which the Sung poet described the plight of the lower classes was most likely a result of the weakening of class lines and an increase of social mobility brought about by the disappearance of the T'ang aristocracy and the more thorough implementation of the civil service examination system. Many of the high officials and famous literary figures of Sung China were of middle class and even rich peasant origins, so during their youths they had opportunities to observe rural conditions at firsthand and in many cases directly engage in rural labor. In the realm of philosophy this broadening of society led to a much wider extension of such basic Confucian terms as "humanity" (*jen*). In earlier Confucian thought, human love was supposed to be graded, but the eleventh-century thinker Chang Tsai (1020–1077) could write: "Heaven is my father and earth is my mother. . . . All people are from the same womb as I, and all things are my companions."[67] Chang Tsai was probably influenced by the Buddhist doctrine of the infinitely compassionate *bodhisattva* in this respect, and the feeling of compassion toward all human beings caused a poet such as Yang Wan-li to identify with the joys and sorrows of the common man:

Watching the Planting

How can we bear hearing of drought two years out of three?
As soon as everything's ripe, all the villages
    will celebrate.
Day after day, this old fellow plays with the field water,
While his eyes watch the blue waves turn to yellow
    clouds of grain.[68]

In such a poem Yang is not using the peasant as a vehicle for political protest, nor is he attempting to escape into a make-believe world of rustic simplicity. His identification with the whole range of humanity inspires the intense joy he feels in watching the rice harvest come to a successful conclusion.

The expanded view of humanity which permeated Sung society enabled a great poet such as Yang to realize that the accomplishments of the common man were as valid as the refined arts of the scholar-officials:

Inns by the Side of the Road

There are two or three country inns by the side of the road;
So early in the morning they don't have hot water,
    much less tea.
Some say these people don't appreciate "art,"[69]
But they've arranged purple myrtle flowers in a
    blue porcelain vase![70]

We have already seen that Yang's friend Yu Mou doubted the validity of a rigid distinction between great and minor poetry, and in this poem Yang shows that he can appreciate the artistic impulse in anyone regardless of his class background.

The more realistic tone of his social protest poetry and his more personal involvement in peasant life are highly attractive aspects of

Yang's rural poetry, but the most delightful innovation he and his contemporaries made was the description of everyday life in the Chinese countryside. Historians have bemoaned the supposed lack of material on peasant life in Chinese historical sources, but if they would only turn to the poetry of Yang and his contemporaries, they would find an abundance of reliable material for the Southern Sung period. Yang Wan-li was fascinated by the various festivals which broke the monotony of peasant life:

Watching a Small Boy Play at Beating the Spring Ox[71]

The little boy lashes his whip and hits the clay ox;
He imitates father "beating spring," hitting its head first.
The brown ox has brown hooves and a pair of white horns;
The herding lad a green raincoat with a rain hat of
    blue bamboo.[72]
This year the soil should be fertile from the rain;
Last year wasn't as happy as this year will be.
When the boy hears of a good harvest, he's happy he
    won't starve;
But when the ox hears of it, he's worried he won't have
    time to get fat.
Soon they will see wheat tassles turn to clouds of brooms;
The paddy rice, too, will fill gallons with its pearls.[73]
When the big fields are all plowed, they'll plow
    the hills;
When will the yellow ox get any rest from now on?[74]

The new realism we have noted in Yang's protest poetry is now used in a totally apolitical fashion, and it is obvious that Yang sees the peasant as something more than a political weather vane.

The highly realistic vignettes of peasant life which Yang has left us could only be the result of detailed personal observation:

Planting Rice Song

The peasant man throws the seedlings and his wife catches;
The little son pulls up the seedlings, while the eldest plants.
The bamboo hat is the peasant's helmet, the raincoat
    his armor,
But the rain soaks him from his head down to his shoulders.
His wife calls him for breakfast and to rest half a minute;

> But he lowers his head, bends his waist, and doesn't
> pay attention.
> "The seedling roots aren't firm, and the bundles aren't wrapped,[75]
> So hold back those goslings and baby ducks!"[76]

Although Yang may be idealizing the peasant slightly by referring to his "helmet" and "armor," he is not painting a picture of "titans of the soil" but of real people whom he had actually observed at work.

We have already observed Yang's interest in the world of children, and peasant children were included, too:

Herding Boys at An-le Fang

> The boy in front pulls an ox across the stream water,
> While the boy in back rides his ox, turning around to
> ask something.
> One boy plays a flute, flowers pinned on his rain hat;
> One ox carries a boy, as she leads her calf along.
> The tender water in the spring stream is pure without silt;
> Fine grasses on spring islets, azure jade without blemish.
> Five oxen wander far off, but the children don't bother them,
> For the boys' home lies there, just across the stream.
> Suddenly a few drops of rain fall on their heads;
> Three rain hats and four raincoats go scurrying off.[77]

Yang's highly realistic description of the activities of the peasant boys is typical of the other peasant poetry translated so far, but this particular poem demonstrates the very fine line between everyday life and the absolute, which was a basic doctrine of the Ch'an Buddhists and certainly one reason for Yang's fascination with the ordinary world.

One could probably justify taking Yang's work as just another example of his rural poetry, as Western art critics have failed to find any special symbolism in the numerous paintings of children riding on water buffaloes or of peasants leading their oxen through their fields.[78] However, any Sung intellectual familiar with Ch'an Buddhist literature would immediately associate Yang's poem and the paintings with one of the most widely known Ch'an parables of Sung times. During the Sung dynasty, a Ch'an master painted a series of ten paintings in which he compared the Ch'an monk's search for enlightenment to a young boy's search for a lost water buffalo. Eventually, the boy finds the water buffalo's tracks, catches the animal,

and rides it back home. After arriving home, the boy forgets about
the buffalo and next both boy and buffalo are forgotten, just as the
Ch'an monk must eventually forget both his goal of *nirvāna* and
himself in order to become enlightened. Finally, in the final picture
of the series, the subject enters the world of everyday life, and the
poem written to accompany the painting says: "Breast exposed, feet
bare, I enter the market place;/ Smeared with dirt and ashes, a smile
covers my face."[79] A comment to the poem reads: "I turn aside from
the tracks of previous sages. Carrying a gourd as I enter the market
or returning to my hut with my staff in hand, I cause all in the bars
and fish shops to attain Buddha-hood."[80] On one level Yang's poem
is a highly realistic description of herding boys bringing their oxen
back home, but on another level the poem can be seen as an allegory
for the ultimate truths of Ch'an.[81] Yet for the Ch'an Buddhists,
there is no need to speak of two levels, for to them the two levels are
identical.

CHAPTER 6

The World of Nature

I Nature in General

WITHOUT a doubt, the most important theme of Sung poetry, and possibly of Chinese poetry in general, is nature. Nature has played a more important role in Chinese civilization than in any other culture, and even in the earliest poems of the *Classic of Poetry* (seventh century B.C. and earlier), one discovers a constant awe for the huge variety of plants and animals and the mysterious processes of birth and death. A few centuries after the *Classic of Poetry*, the love of nature became one of the fundamental bases of Chou dynasty Taoist thought, which emphasized the total harmony between man and his environment. Under the influence of neo-Taoism, such fourth-century writers as T'ao Ch'ien and Hsieh Ling-yün abandoned the courtly topics of Han dynasty authors and wrote the first pure nature poetry China had known. In India, Buddhism had not been associated with any special cult of nature, but when the religion reached China, it picked up the Chinese love of natural objects, and as a result, many of the most famous monasteries were built in such beauty spots as Mount Lu or the T'ien-t'ai Mountains. Buddhist themes gradually filtered into Chinese nature poetry, and by the seventh century, the great nature poet and landscape painter Wang Wei (701–761) took his literary name Mo-chieh from the renowned Indian Buddhist layman Vimalakīrti (Chinese *Wei-mo-chieh*).

Although the world of man still held a very important place in Yang's poetry, he followed current interest in natural topics. The reasons for Yang's love of nature were many, for in addition to the pure sensuous delight he felt in surveying a grand landscape, there were significant intellectual and spiritual factors to be considered, too. In fact, we frequently find that Yang seems to enter a trance at

103

times when he views a particularly outstanding stretch of scenery.
When crossing the famed Po-yang Lake he wrote:

On the Thirteenth of the Fourth Month I Cross Lake Po-yang[1]

In the middle of the lake there is a mountain called Mount K'ang-lang,
shaped like a leach floating on the water.

I anchor the boat at Prince Po's Lake,[2]
For there is wind and rain until midnight.
Though I want to cross, dare I be too self-confident?
Idle safety is all that I wish.
I know there's no use in lone sadness;
So I endure a while, continuously sighing.
The night is long, and suddenly I fall asleep;
I'm so exhausted, I don't even know it's dawn.
The boatmen call me to get up;
There's a favorable wind and no room for delay.
With half an oar-stroke we're already at mid-lake;
Our boat like a single leaf on a mirror's surface.
I look up and see the clouds' robes open;
I glance sideways as the sail's belly fills.
The sky is like a glazed bell,
Which covers over this crystal cup below.
The waves' reflection—squirting gold juice;
The sun's rays—penetrating silver pillars.
Mount K'ang is a leach in a cup;
Mount Lu a curtain in front of our sail.[3]
Suddenly the earth has no support;
Everything's hazy like a shoreless sea.
My body seems to become void and empty;
Riding the air, I wander far and wide.
At first I worried we'd crash against perilous waves;
I didn't expect to take in this marvelous scene.
During the last six summers and winters
I've passed to and fro on this water three times.
Before crossing, my mind is never at ease;
But while I cross, I always enjoy it.
I'm tired of wandering and ought to go home;
And not just because of the apes' and cranes' complaints![4]

The poem starts out ordinarily enough, and one suspects he is about
to hear a lamentation about the tribulations of the scholar-official

who is forever on the road. Yet as soon as the boat reaches midlake, Yang seems to enter a realm separate from the ordinary world of perception. The boat is dwarfed by the immensity of the lake and appears to be a small leaf gliding on the surface of a mirror. Suddenly the entire world is magically transformed, the sky turning into a "glazed bell" and the lake into a "crystal cup," while ordinary water and sunlight are transmuted into gold and silver. Yang then leaves the support of the earth behind and ascends into a world of mist and haze which is completely without directions or limits. His body like a void, he rides on the winds, totally free from any connection with mundane existence. The element of flying in Yang's description of his trancelike state sounds suspiciously Taoist, but when he tells us his body has changed to a void, he is most likely referring to the Buddhist doctrine of *śunyatā*, or emptiness of phenomenal existence. In any case, the distinction between Taoism and Buddhism in such a poem is extremely nebulous, because a Sung poet would not have recognized sharp differences between the mystical experiences of both philosophies.

Whether we care to emphasize the Buddhist or Taoist elements in Yang's poem, his description of a mystical experience in natural surroundings bears a strong resemblance to many of the scenes one sees in the landscape painting of Yang's contemporaries. Although landscape painting had started in the North-south Period, and continued to develop in the T'ang dynasty, it was generally ranked as a lower form of art and did not become the dominant style of painting in China until the Five Dynasties just before Sung times.[5] Whereas the world of man had dominated T'ang and earlier art, in Southern Sung paintings we find the scholar-official lost in the contemplation of mountain peaks or other natural objects. Frequently the facial expressions of these men are hidden from our view, but when we can see their faces, we usually notice that they seem to be in a tranquil trancelike state. A particularly magnificent painting by the thirteenth-century painter Ma Lin depicts two old men staring vacantly at a thundering waterfall in front of them.[6] Although the two men stand together, there is no communication between them, for they are totally absorbed in their meditation on the mountain cataract. One reason they watch the ever-changing water is because it is a symbol of the constant flux of the universe, the impermanent *saṁsāra* of the Buddhists. But, perhaps, even more important, complete identification with the natural objects around them enables the men to be freed of the ego (Sanskrit *atman,* Chinese *wo*), the grasping of which is the major obstacle to enlightenment. We have seen how Yang's body became "void" when he was lost in the beauties of Lake Po-yang, and similarly the painters of his age lost their egos in the vastness of mountains and water. The reason for the Sung artists' reduction of the size of man in relation to his natural surroundings was not necessarily to remind him of how insignificant he is alongside nature, but rather to free him from the egotistical attachment to self.

What sort of nature was it in which the Chinese poet and painter wished to lose himself? The Confucian believed that there was an ethical order behind nature which expresses itself in the successive changes of the mandate of heaven in past political history. This view of nature could be twisted to justify superstitious belief in portents and omens from heaven, but it could also lead to the Sung neo-Confucian doctrine of the "investigation of things," *ko-wu,* through which one explored the ethical structure of nature by carefully examining natural and human phenomena. The major alternative to the moralistic Confucian view of nature in early Chinese thought was Taoism, which is typified by Lao-tzu's affirmation that "heaven and earth are not humane."[7] Such a doctrine does not mean that nature is necessarily harmful to mankind, but that the Confucian view of an ethically structured universe is a delusion, and nature is totally impartial to human activities.

Despite the more usual Confucian and Taoist views of nature, there have been times when Chinese poets firmly believed in the complete hostility of nature to man. In late T'ang times such pessimism reached a high point, and poets like Li Ho (791–817), Han Yü,[8] and Lu T'ung (d. 835)[9] considered nature to be largely malevolent in its attitude toward mankind. In his well-known poem "Don't Go Out the Door," Li Ho wrote: "Heaven is deceptive; the earth, secretive./ The bear viper devours men's souls;/ Snow and frost snap our bones."[10]

In a poem by Yang Wan-li, we see a universe which is not as violent as Li Ho's but almost equally hostile:

Chanting Bitterly

The ants have no autumn clothes, while the geese
have fur coats;

Yet hunting for food under a frosty heaven, both of
    them are sad.
The goose calls as it dies of cold, honking continuously;
The ant's knees, frozen stiff, move, then stop.
The master chants bitterly as the day gets late,
And an old servant comes, pressing him to eat breakfast.
My little boy is reciting his books; I call, but he
    doesn't come;
While on the table our yellow leek noodles grow cold.[11]

Although nature seems to lack compassion for her creatures, the domestic scene portrayed in Yang's work lends a human touch missing from Li Ho's poem. The cold weather depresses Yang Wan-li, but the natural forces do not overwhelm him, as can be seen even more clearly in a much later poem on a similar theme:

A Later Song About Suffering from the Cold

The white gull stands in snow, his ankles pierced by cold;
The pelicans avoid wind, unable to fly straight.
A pair of wild ducks makes a fool of the evening cold;
They float and dive in the icy river—who can figure that out?
But most of all I love our red boat with its boatmen;[12]
Green raincoats, purple bamboo caps, they haul the
    fanged mast.
I worry my fingers will fall off or ears peel away;
Even the rushes' flowers don't have any place to hide.
I send riders ahead to buy some dry firewood,
And soon I'm warming by a blazing fire, giving myself a roast.
It's so cold even the three-footed raven sun won't
    come out;[13]
I gaze at the clouds, complaining to heaven, but heaven
    doesn't cry.[14]

Once again nature's creatures are deserted to fend for themselves, and when in the last line Yang states "heaven doesn't cry" he is echoing Lao-tzu's assertion of nature's inhumanity. Yet the nature in this poem is hardly as hostile as that found in Li Ho's works, for the ducks seem to resist the cold with little difficulty, and despite the somewhat chilly ride in a boat, Yang is entertained by the picturesque clothing of the boatmen. Most important of all, Yang allows himself to reminisce about the hardships of the journey while roasting himself at a blazing fire.

Another poem of the same title further emphasizes the feeling of cosiness which Yang allows us even during the most hostile winter weather:

Suffering from the Cold
(First Poem of Three)

When I dread the heat, I think of snow whirling around me;
Suffering from cold, I wish the willows would bring back spring.
As evening comes, the setting sun has little warmth,
So even its reflection on my west window is nice![15]

In this poem we feel that our suffering is relative, for during the hot summer season we yearn for the cold which winter brings us. No matter how cold the weather is, we can always escape into comfortable domestic surroundings to avoid the wind's blast and enjoy what little heat the sun gives us. The late T'ang poets such as Li Ho were extreme in their pessimistic view of nature, but their attitude toward life and nature was only an intensification of the generally melancholy mood which prevailed among Chinese intellectuals from at least the fourth century to roughly the tenth century. The Sung poets rejected the view that the world is hostile to man, and Chinese literature was never the same again.

II Landscape

Now that we have discussed Yang Wan-li's attitude to nature in general, let us explore his treatment of the most important aspect of nature described by Chinese poets, namely, the landscape. Here again we shall find a knowledge of contemporary painting useful, so we must first say something about the evolution of landscape painting in China before and during the twelfth century. The Five Dynasties and Northern Sung artists considered the landscape to be the highest form of painting, and as a result it took precedence over the interest in court and Buddhist religious pictures which had dominated earlier T'ang painting. The great Northern Sung masters Fan K'uan[16] and Kuo Hsi,[17] both of whom lived in the early eleventh century, developed a highly original monochrome ink style in which huge, towering mountain peaks completely dwarf human beings and their activities.[18] Particularly in Kuo Hsi's masterpieces the wildly undulating mountain peaks take on a life of their own which seems to render the human world totally superfluous in the scheme of the universe.[19] It is hardly surprising that much of the landscape poetry of the Northern Sung bears a strong resemblance to such painting, and Kuo Hsi's near contemporary Su Shih writes:

> I only see the two cliffs, green, green, obscured in
> precipitous gorges;
> In their midst, springs soar forth from a hundred paths.
> Threading woods, tying rocks, they are hidden yet reappear,
> Racing down to valley mouths, where they become swift streams.[20]

Despite the undeniable grandeur of the Northern Sung paintings, one can hardly avoid feeling that these landscapes are too cold and remote to allow the ordinary mortal to linger long in the wild and untamed nature which they depict. In fact, Chinese artists soon tired of these superhuman landscapes, and the generation in which Yang lived saw a complete revolution in the art of landscape painting. The end result of this upheaval was the creation of the Ma-Hsia style which dominated Chinese art for the rest of the twelfth century until it, too, was eventually overturned by the Yüan masters.

A brief description of the Ma-Hsia style would be useful, because it will aid us in understanding the innovations Yang Wan-li made in the field of landscape poetry. Although the two principal members of the school, Ma Yüan (fl. 1190–1230)[21] and Hsia Kuei (fl. 1190–1230),[22] lived in the generation immediately following Yang, the changeover to a new style was well under way during Yang's lifetime, so we shall take the liberty of referring directly to the works of the two great masters themselves. In the typical landscape of the Ma-Hsia school one is immediately impressed by the great simplification of forms by the use of sharp, angular brush strokes, which impart a calligraphic quality to much of the painting.[23] This more abstract quality is in great contrast to the more luxuriant detail and "realism" in the painting of rocks and trees in Northern Sung landscape. Although there is little direct literary proof, it is very tempting to suggest that the greater abstraction in the Southern Sung landscape painters is influenced by Northern and Southern Sung Ch'an painters who attempted to convey the immediacy of sudden enlightenment through the simplicity of their painting.[24]

However, the stylistic characteristics of the Ma-Hsia landscape are of less interest to us than the actual content of the paintings. The typical Ma-Hsia landscape consists of gently sloping mountains

bathed partially in a sea of white mist and clouds. Human habita-
tions are usually present and human beings are to be seen strolling
through the mountain scenery. The most striking feature of such
paintings is that for the first time in the Sung dynasty the landscape
is reduced to human terms, for the overpowering crags of Kuo Hsi
and Li Ch'eng (tenth century) are completely eliminated, and
nothing is allowed to interrupt the smooth contours of distant mountains. One feels that one could comfortably walk about in a Ma-Hsia
landscape, and, in fact, their works are much more heavily populated than the Northern Sung paintings. The mist and clouds never
suggest the possibility of a violent storm and merely heighten the
effect of tranquility by smoothing out any of the rough contours to
be found in nature. In many of Ma Yüan's paintings there is an
undeniable "sweetness," which has appealed greatly to Westerners
but was violently rejected by the Yüan masters. In summary, the
Ma-Hsia landscape is, at least on the surface, a friendly sort of place
meant precisely for scholar-officials such as Yang Wan-li.[25]
    This friendly quality of the Ma-Hsia landscape can be seen in a
poem in which Yang describes a mountain which could easily be an
inhabitant of their paintings:

As my Boat Passes Goose Walk River Mouth, I Gaze at Chicken Coop
                        Mountain in Ho-chou

    For two months the green mountains haven't left me
        for even a while;
    But when I enter the city I don't ever see mountains
        at all.
    A myriad peaks have already gone back after sending me off;
    Only Chicken Coop Mountain isn't willing to leave.[26]

    It would be difficult for a painting to express the human qualities
of nature as explicitly as a poem, and Yang emphasizes these human
qualities by personifying the landscape to an extent never seen
before in Chinese verse:

As I Cook Breakfast at New Grove, I Gaze on Bell Mountain

    I took leave of Bell Mountain a month ago,
    So how does he recognize my carriage returning north?
    We don't know each other's names, yet he's very polite,
    For he suddenly arrives at the side of New Grove's inn![27]

If we compare this poem with a famous verse of Li Po, Yang's striking originality in the Chinese literary tradition comes into sharper focus:

Sitting Alone by Ching-t'ing Mountain

Flocks of birds, flying high, have all disappeared;
A solitary cloud drifts by leisurely, on its own.
We never grow tired of looking at each other;
There is Ching-t'ing Mountain alone.[28]

Although Li Po speaks of a kind of companionship with the mountain, his poem is actually a study of his own solitude, which is heightened by eliminating all of the birds and allowing only a solitary cloud to drift by. Li's relation to the mountain is quite different from Yang's, for Li seems to delight more in his own solitary splendor than in any companionship with the mountain, and although the mountain and he continue to eye one another, their friendship is as cold and aloof as Li Po's relations with his contemporaries. On the other hand, Yang's mountain is endowed with all of the human qualities of the Sung scholar, for although he does not know Yang's name or social position, he still has a genuine interest in forming a close friendship. Yang's mountain is not one of the craggy peaks of the painter Kuo Hsi but rather one of the subdued slopes of the Southern Sung Ma-Hsia school.

Yang's feeling of a close personal relationship with the natural objects around him is equally apparent in a most remarkable work about the sunrise:

The Ballad of Hsi-E

In the middle of autumn I spent the night at Pi-hsieh City. When I got up early in the morning, the dawn star had already risen, and the sun was about to come up, but the moon had not set yet. The scenery went through a myriad changes. Since this is probably the most spectacular sight in the world, I wrote "The Ballad of Hsi-E" to record it.

Hsi Ho, the sun god, wakes from his dreams, wants to
    get up and go,
So his purple gold raven lets loose with a croak.[29]
The cry falls from heaven into the world of men,

And in a thousand villages, a myriad hamlets, all
  cocks compete in crowing.
The White Moon-beauty hurries west, but she hasn't
  quite gone home;[30]
She shakes her silver platter, scouring it in the wind
  and dew.
Then a jade pellet star comes flying from the east,[31]
And knocks down her cassia groves and snow-furred hare.[32]
Who has curtained off half the sky with a red brocade?[33]
Red light and vermillion vapor permeate mountains
  and rivers.
In a moment the sun drives his cinnabar colored wheels[34]
Up into the cold void, crushing the azure jade sky.
This old poet has already walked over ten miles,
So who says that the sun god is the first guy up?[35]

Such a lengthy description of the rising sun is extremely rare in the
Chinese literary tradition, but the most original feature of the poem
is the way in which Yang personifies the heavenly bodies. In the
poem "As I Cook Breakfast at New Grove, I Gaze at Bell Mountain", Yang personified a mountain by describing it as a friendly
Sung scholar, but in this poem Yang uses a totally different device.
Through the medium of Chinese popular mythology the sun becomes the sun god, Hsi Ho, and the moon the White Moon Beauty,
Su E. The use of popular mythology to give human qualities to the
heavenly bodies, brings the mysteries of the celestial transformations down to a level more comprehensible to the human mind.
Moreover, Yang shows himself to be just one more human being
among the anthropomorphic sun, moon, and stars, so that the
human qualities of seemingly inaccessible bodies allows him to joke
with them and suggest that he is even more industrious than the sun
god himself.
  Yang was justly delighted by his new treatment of the sunrise, for
he wrote another poem on the subject of the moon in the early
morning hours, which utilizes many of the same devices of the
previous poem:

I Enter the East Ministry Early in the Morning When
The Waning Moon Has Just Risen[36]

Lamp in hand, I rush to the Library's office;
On both sides of the street, doors are still shut.

The White Moon-beauty alone has risen early;
Her black dish is washed in heaven's azure pool.
Like a precious button scraped so you see its lacquer,
Her silver remains on only half of one edge.
Suddenly her eyes turn from black to white;[37]
She opens them wide and gives me a cross stare.
A black mist penetrates her pupils;
She sneaks a glance, for she dares not be open.
Glistening white, a single jade plum star[38]
Moves before her, guiding her whirling wheel.
Twinkling bright, a few golden grains
Follow her chariot's dust in escort.
The morning cock crows three times,
And the capital's riders contend in their race.
The stars' rays have almost totally vanished,
While the moon's shadow is pale, hardly a trace.
Then the Gold Raven Sun flies up into the heavens
And spits forth his red dragon scales![39]

Once again Yang uses popular mythology to personify the heavenly
bodies, but in this poem the moon is even more human than in the
previous work, and she could easily pass for some Chinese coquette
of the Sung period. The great originality of Yang's description of the
moon can be understood if we compare it to a standard anthology
piece of Li Po:

Drinking Alone Beneath the Moon

Amidst the flowers with a jug of wine,
I drink alone without any friends.
Raising my cup, I invite the moon,
So with my shadow and me, we are three.
The moon does not know how to drink,
And my shadow merely follows my body in vain.
For a while I accompany moon and shadow;
Enjoying yourself, you should keep pace with spring.
When I sing, the moon hesitates;
I dance, and my shadow scatters.
When sober, let us share our joy;
Drunk, we will go our own ways.
Let us bind ourselves in passionless wanderings,
And meet again far off in the Milky Way.[40]

Once again, the solitude of the T'ang intellectual sets the mood of his poem. Although Li, his shadow, and the moon seem to be three companions, they are actually totally isolated from each other, with the moon aloof from Li's drinking and his shadow dispersing whenever he moves. The three can only engage in "passionless wanderings" and their future meeting is delayed to the remote Milky Way. In contrast, Yang's moon is a real goddess who flirts with him like some Sung beauty. For Li the natural phenomena are aloof and cold, but for Yang the surrounding landscape is endowed with real human qualities.

We have already referred to the "sweetness" of many of the Ma-Hsia landscape paintings, and the seductive coyness of Yang's moon in the previous poem is quite similar to the velvety softness which a painter such as Ma Yüan uses to lure the observer into his pictures. Yang's mountains, too, are equally capable of teasing the poet as the moon did:

The Boat Passes An-jen
(Second Poem of Five)

At first I loved you distant mountains for presenting
    me this painting;
But suddenly you rolled it up, dim as if it no longer existed.
Don't try to cheat my old eyes, for they're still clear;
Even with all your fog and smoke, I still can count you![41]

In the same way that the moon beauty plays hard to get, the mountains attempt to hide themselves in a bank of clouds and mist. The same coy behavior can be observed in another group of mountains:

Crossing Flower Bridge at Dawn, I Enter the Boundary
of Hsüan-chou
(First Poem of Four)

As the road enters Hsüan-ch'eng, the mountains get
    even stranger;
Like blue dragons they race furiously; green phoenixes,
    they fly.
This poet's eyes are pretty sharp, and I've already
    got a peek,
But they still rush to pull up their clouds into a
    kingfisher-colored curtain.[42]

Yang's mountains are as seductive as some coquette who allows her lover a small peek of her beauty and then hastily covers herself up.

In addition to resembling the Southern Sung landscape in their seductive sweetness, Yang's mountain vistas follow the Ma-Hsia school in creating the coy effect through the use of heavy cloud cover through which the mountains are alternately hidden and revealed. Of course, clouds and fog occur frequently in earlier Chinese painting, but the Southern Sung artists went to the extreme of commonly leaving more of the painting in mist than is filled with detail. As a result of so much cloud cover, we find that the Southern Sung landscape is almost as inaccessible to the viewer as the towering crags of the Northern Sung artists.[43] Thus, we are presented with a seemingly unresolvable paradox in which the coy mountains of the Ma-Hsia school seem to invite exploration but actually keep far away when one attempts to approach them.

That the seemingly friendly mountain peaks are ultimately inaccessible to the scholar official is made clear in the following landscape poem:

Passing Hsieh Family Bay

Having walked all the cow trails and rabbit paths,
I suddenly meet a flat waste, joining the sky on all sides.
My thoughts follow white herons, flying off in pairs;
My eyes pass the green mountains with their millions of folds.
I've already seen the near ranges, so I look at the far ones;
I don't love the interlocking peaks, only the solitary ones.
One hill, then a gorge, I wonder what they mean by *that*;
For they keep all us officials away and welcome only
    herding boys![44]

In this work Yang is rambling about one of the friendly domesticated landscapes of the Ma-Hsia artists, rather than straining to scale one of the forbidding peaks of Kuo Hsi. As his eyes follow the flight of the herons, his line of vision leaves the human world behind and contemplates the myriad transformations of the mountain ranges; yet, despite the fact that these mountains seem to beckon him on, he knows that they are inaccessible to him. It is highly significant that only the herding boys can reach the mountain peaks, for in earlier Chinese poetry rural characters such as farmers, woodsmen, and fishermen had always been seen as symbols for the realm beyond the ordinary world of dust. The meaning of Yang's poem is that the mountains are only accessible to rural people who have divested themselves of worldly preoccupations of the official life and have rejected the rational intellectualism of the Confucian scholar-official.

Not only does nature remain aloof from human beings, despite the external deception of friendliness, but it also seems to take a perverse delight in causing difficulties for no reason at all:

Spring Cold

Wind and sun, clear weather and heat, all come together;
Peach flowers report to me that the plums are blossoming.
As soon as you've discarded all your robes and furs,
The spring cold will come back at midnight just on purpose![45]

Although Yang has put his winter clothes away, the spring cold insists on troubling him to put them back on again.

In the previous poem Yang is able to protect himself from nature's delight in causing him trouble, but in the next he is not so able to escape from his problems:

On the Road to Wan-ling

This creek twists like a pair of robe belts;
The bridge is as bushy as a centipede.[46]
Sound on the umbrella—rain in the pine path;
Shadow of nests—wind over a willow pond.
A dog follows this traveler by mistake;
And an ox *insists* I'm his herding boy.[47]
I'm in a rush and don't want to go slowly,
But just try hurrying along a road that's slippery![48]

The road is a quagmire due to the rain, making travel extremely difficult, but the country animals compound Yang's troubles by insisting on following him around. Their pursuit of him might even take on elements of the surrealistic if it were not for the good humor with which Yang faces nature's mischief.

Although the perverseness of nature is directed against all human beings, the most sensitive of humans, the poet, suffers the most:

Setting Off at Silver Tree Grove

Don't cross the stream's bridge at Silver Tree Grove,
For the creek isn't nearly so deep as the road's mud.
A gust of pure wind steals across my face,
While fair weather, only half revealed, worries my
    traveler's heart.
Far ranges provoke the clouds into snowing in autumn,
And the pale sky, brushed with ink, darkens at dawn.
So many good poems struggle to throw themselves at me,
But willows snatch and flowers steal; where can I find them?[49]

Once again Yang is impeded by mud on the rain-soaked road and mountain ranges "provoke" the clouds into snowing. Good poems want to burst out of the poet in line with his Ch'an spontaneity, but the willows and flowers conspire against him and steal the poems before he can write them down.

In the last three poems we have seen that although nature seems to be approachable on the surface, it is actually engaged in a giant "conspiracy" against mankind. We must not confuse this "conspiracy of nature," one of the commonest themes in Yang's poetry, with the late T'ang view that nature is basically malevolent toward mankind. Although nature delights in exasperating mankind, it goes about its activities in a reasonably good-humored manner. This combination of gentleness and aloofness is admirably summarized in a couplet written on a painting by Ma Yüan entitled *Walking on a Mountain Path in Spring:* "Brushing against his sleeves, wild flowers dance by themselves;/ Avoiding the man, secluded birds do not sing."[50] The scholar-official who walks through this landscape is charmed by the flowers which seem to embrace him in friendship, yet the birds fly away from him and the line of his vision is lost in the emptiness of fog-enshrouded mountains.

Other than attempting to vex poets such as Yang Wan-li, why does nature engage in the "conspiracy" against mankind? Specifically, what is nature trying to hide from human view? The *Tao-te ching* hints at an answer when it describes the *Tao* or basic principle underlying nature in the following terms: "It is the Mystery of mysteries,/ The gate of the multitude of marvels."[51] The *Lotus Sūtra* describes the mysteries of the absolute truth of the Buddha in similar terms. "The knowledge of the Buddhas is extremely profound and limitless. The gate of their knowledge is difficult to comprehend or enter. No *śvavakas* or *pratyeka-buddhas* can know it."[52] The spiritual ancestor of all nature poets in China, T'ao Yüan-ming, wrote the following while describing a magnificent landscape: "In all of this there is a fundamental truth;/ I want to explain it but have already forgotten the words."[53]

Yang Wan-li develops T'ao Yüan-ming's theme of the ineffable mystery hiding behind the outward appearances of nature in the following poem:

> After a Rain, I Get up at Dawn to Look at the Mountains
>
> At morning, when I go out of my bramble door,
> The peak across the river seems to have changed.
> Yet I look at it closely, still the same old mountain;
> Only its color is different from yesterday.
> Although it passed through last night's rain,
> There's no need for this to have such an effect.
> The Cloud Master grasps all of the mountains
> And places them in the middle of blue water.
> Their sand and soil become green and float;
> Their grass and trees increase in luxuriance.
> They are approaching the decay of autumn,
> So how could they regain their spring looks?
> The meaning of this is certainly not shallow,
> And they use it to make fun of this old poet.
> This could all be resolved with one word,
> But unfortunately my words are unskilled.
> Even if my words were skilled enough,
> They wouldn't be so deep as the mountain's colors.[54]

The transformations which Yang witnesses cannot be described in mere human language, for like the truth of Ch'an enlightenment, they are incomprehensible to the dualistic reasoning process of man.

For Yang Wan-li the creations of nature seem continually to expound the mysteries behind the Buddhist doctrine:

> A Pair of Pagodas at Orchid Creek
>
> The tall pagoda isn't pointed, the small pagoda is;
> One wears a brocade cassock, the other a silver robe.

> I ask them why they don't ever talk,
> But they have the rapids speak for the Buddha.[55]

In other words, the natural creations express the truths of Buddhism better than the artificial temples that mankind constructs.

Another landscape poem gives us further clues of how Yang's Buddhist interests related to much of his nature poetry:

> I Break Out in Song While Spending the Night at East Bank
> (Third Poem of Three)

> The Lord of Heaven wants to fill my poet's eyes,
> But he's worried lest the autumn mountains be too
>   withered, insipid.
> So suddenly he tailors Shu brocade and spreads out
>   crimson clouds of Wu;[56]
> Low, low, he rubs them on autumn mountains halfway up.
> In a second he turns the red brocade into kingfisher gauze;
> His loom weaves out ravens returning home at evening.
> Suddenly, evening ravens and kingfisher gauze disappear,
> And all I see is the clear river pure as silk.[57]

Yang compares the changes in the scenery to magical weaving done by the major deity of Chinese folk religion, thus bringing the transformations down to a more "human" level for men to understand. The deity creates an exquisite tapestry from the evening sunset, but suddenly this heavenly handiwork vanishes and, in a flash of enlightenment, Yang perceives "the clear river pure as silk." Yang's sudden enlightenment is not only spiritual but it also occurs on the poetic level, too, for the last line of the poem is a direct quotation from Hsieh T'iao (464–499) and one of the most famous lines of Chinese poetry, considered the height of poetic achievement by T'ang and Sung poets. Meditation on the miraculous transformations of the landscape has wiped aside the illusory creations of the Lord of Heaven and brought sudden enlightenment in a vision of a "clear river pure as silk."

One could object that such an interpretation of Yang's poem is a bit too forced if he had not left us a work in which he leaves no doubt about the Buddhist symbolism he discovered in the mountain landscape:

Morning was bright and clear but suddenly fog arose. When it had
stopped and the sun came out, the scenery became strange and unusual.

Setting out at morning, I gazed at the far-off mountains;
They were so clear, you could count them one by one.
But as the desire to gaze at them springs up in this recluse,
He incurs the jealousy of the mountain spirits.
Retreating, they display their spiritual powers,[58]
Their transformations are startling, frightening.
At first they take *tūla* tree cotton[59]
And split it open into fluffy white gauze.
Surrounding all, it envelops the world;
Looking up, I lose sight of heaven's vault.
On high hangs a red crystal platter,[60]
Measuring no more than a yard across.
It shines down midst the empty mist,
Red rays piercing this light silk.
In the middle are shadows of men and animals;
Confused and disorderly, they race back and forth.
Each of them seems to be grasping at something,
But I can't distinguish what it is.
As if I didn't think it strange enough,
Even weirder things begin to happen now.
Along the road pennants stand like pearls;
In surrounding mountains trees are ranked like jasper.
Across the sky stretches a golden bridge;
A jade *stūpa* looms from the ground.[61]
My startled eyes have just gotten a close look,
When it's rolled up from the ground and hidden away.
Dazed and in doubt, I rub my eyes;
I still see the old mountain road in front.
How can I know whether it is illusion or reality:
I can't determine whether I'm dreaming or awake.
The spirits wander on Mount E-mei,[62]
Cheating the vulgar and laughing at old man Buddha.
You who cheat and laugh are laughed at, too,
For old man Buddha is laughing at you.[63]

The description that Yang gives of the mountain landscape is very
similar to the earlier poems we have read, but his explicit references
to Buddhist terminology and ideas help us to understand the relationship between the landscape and Yang's Ch'anist beliefs. As is
usual, the mountain peaks start out being perfectly visible to the

poet, and as he counts them one by one, he forms a personal acquaintance with them as if they were good friends. In this sense, the mystery of the landscape seems to be fairly accessible to the human intellect, and the mountains fit into the Ma-Hsia mold of a friendly, human landscape. However, just as in the Ma-Hsia landscapes, nature conspires against the observer and soon the mountains are shrouded in mist. This perverse humor of the mountain spirits hides the processes of transformation from the poet, for the god displays his magical powers much as Māra, Śakra, or other Indian deities do in Buddhist *sūtras*. Yang's reference to men racing about in fog and grasping at phantom objects suggests that he viewed the fog and mist as an allegory for the insubstantial world of illusion in which men delude themselves by grasping (Sanskrit *upādāna*, Chinese *ch'ü*) for sensual objects.

Although the fog of illusion has transformed the mountain road beyond recognition, even stranger phenomena occur as the sunlight begins to filter back into the fog, for suddenly a miraculous *stūpa*, or pagoda, appears, crowned by a golden bridge and surrounded by pearl banners and jasper trees. Here Yang is alluding to one of the most famous sections of the *Lotus Sūtra*, the "Stūpa-saṃdarśa-parivartah" (Chinese, "Chien pao-t'a p'in"), or "The Apparition of the Stupa," which describes the appearance of a miraculous *stūpa* during a sermon of the Buddha:

Then from the earth in front of the Buddha gushed forth a *stūpa*, consisting of the seven gems, five hundred *yojanas* high and two hundred fifty *yojanas* in breadth. It stood in the sky and was decorated by all kinds of precious things: five thousand railings and ten million shrines. Adorned by innumerable banners and flags, jeweled garlands were hung on it, with billions of jeweled bells suspended from its top. In all four directions it emitted the fragrance of *tamala* leaves and sandalwood, which filled all the world.[64]

When the disciples of the Buddha saw this phenomenon, they were greatly overjoyed and asked what it portended. The Buddha explained the *stūpa* contained the essential being (Sanskrit *atma-bhāva*, Chinese *ch'üan-shen*) of the Buddha and that the apparition was to appear whenever the true *dharma* was taught: "Whenever there is a place in the nations of the ten directions where the *Sūtra of the Lotus of the Law* is preached, my *stūpa* will gush forth in front for the sake of those listening to this *sūtra*, and in order to be a

witness to them, it will make praise, saying: 'Excellent!' "[65] Buddha
affirms that before his own enlightenment, the apparition of the
stūpa appeared to him and applauded his final awakening. Thus, in
both the Lotus Sūtra and Yang Wan-li's poem, the stūpa is a symbol
for complete enlightenment.

In view of Mahāyānist doctrine, it is quite appropriate that in the
Sūtra and Yang's poem, this enlightenment is symbolized by an
apparition, for to Buddhists there is utterly no duality between
illusion and reality. This is the precise reason why Yang states that
he does not know the difference between illusion and reality, or
whether he is dreaming or awake, for fundamentally the optical
illusion he has just witnessed is no more an illusion than the world of
"common sense" to which he awakes after the fog has dispersed.
The laugh of the Buddha is directed toward those men who continue
to delude themselves in their ignorance of the basic truth spoken by
the Ch'an master Huang Po: "The Buddhas and all the sentient
beings are just one Mind, and there are no other dharmas. . . . This
one Mind is simply the Buddha, and there is absolutely no distinction between the Buddha and the sentient beings."[66]

An understanding of the Buddhist symbolism in Yang's poem is of
great use in explaining his general view of the natural landscape,
and further research would probably show that many of the concepts
which Yang develops could be extended to a general interpretation
of Southern Sung landscape painting and poetry. One of the most
basic ideas in Yang's poetry that we have discussed is the mystery
behind the numerous transformations to be witnessed in a mountain
landscape. In view of the preceding poem, we can conclude that the
mystery of the landscape is for Yang a symbol of the ineffable mystery of Buddhist enlightenment. Just as the mountains seem to be
friendly at first, enlightenment seems easy to obtain to the un-
initiated, but upon further reflection it seems to be impossibly
difficult, just as the mountain appears to be totally inaccessible to
the ordinary intellectual.

And yet, the friendliness of the mountain landscape is not totally
illusory, for although enlightenment *seems* difficult to obtain, it is
actually a simple matter to the enlightened: "The practice of Ch'an
is to be described as the gold and piss method. Before it is understood, it is all gold, but after it is understood, it is all like piss."[67]
The coyness of the mountains symbolizes the paradox in this saying
of a Sung dynasty Ch'an master, namely, enlightenment is both

difficult and easy to obtain. On the one hand, the mountain will come down and greet the poet, while on the other, the mountain will hide himself behind a bank of clouds with a devilish relish for thwarting the enjoyment of human beings. The "conspiracy of nature" is similar to the "conspiracy" of enlightenment, which is both obtainable and unobtainable at any one moment. In the *Asta-sāhāsrikā-prajñā-pāramitā Sūtra* we read: "I say the Buddha's *dharma* is also like an illusion, like a dream. I say that *nirvāna*, too, is like an illusion, like a dream."[68]

Such an interpretation of Yang's poetry can be applied directly to the paintings of the Ma-Hsia school, and very likely to many other Chinese landscape paintings. The mountain peaks which human figures contemplate in a state of mystical ecstasy symbolize the truth of enlightenment, that is, the sole substantial reality behind the world of illusion. Although such mountains as Sumeru have played a very important place in Indian religion, a mountain cult was developed independently in China at least by late Chou times. Literary references to sacrifices for the holy mountains in the early historical texts and artistic remains, such as the *Po-shan-lu,* or incense burners in the shape of mountains populated by fantastic animals, show that in Han times the mountain was already a symbol for otherworldly truth.[69] By the end of the Han dynasty, the importance of rites associated with entering mountains in such works as the *Pao-p'u-tzu* shows that the Han cult of mountains had become connected with the search for immortality of the Taoist alchemists.[70] By the time that Buddhism became firmly entrenched in Chinese thought, the mountain was already a symbol for ultimate truth, so it is no wonder that Buddho-Taoist nature poets such as Hsieh Ling-yün wrote of the enlightenment they had attained midst wild and craggy peaks: "Looking at all this, I forget my concern for objects;/ Suddenly enlightened, I can cast off everything."[71] By the time the Ma-Hsia painters created their landscapes, mountains were already a symbol for the truth that one realizes upon enlightenment.

However, the mountains of reality and substance in the Ma-Hsia paintings are bathed in clouds and mist, and, hence, nearly invisible to us, much as our perception is clouded in the world of illusion. In the *Analects* of Confucius, clouds are already a symbol for inconsequential things of an illusory nature: "Riches and honors are to me as floating clouds."[72] One could write pages on cloud symbolism in Chinese poetry and art, but by the time Buddhist poetry was being

written in China, clouds were frequently taken as a symbol for the
insubstantial world of illusion, and in the T'ang dynasty the Buddhist nature poet Wang Wei wrote:

> I did not know Fragrant Pile Monastery
> And entered several miles into cloud peaks.
> Ancient trees, no paths of men;
> In the deep mountains, whence a bell's sound? . . .[73]

Wang Wei does not know where the temple is located, and to
compound his confusion, he is lost in trackless, cloud-covered
mountains, when suddenly the bell of Buddhist truth awakens him
to where he is. However, there is no need to despair about the
clouds of insubstantial illusion, for in the end they are just as real as
the mountains of substantial reality behind them. When one views a
painting by the Ma-Hsia masters, he soon realizes that the unfilled
areas that represent mist are just as full as the areas covered by
ink.[74] For Yang and all Ch'an Buddhists, reality is identical to illusion and illusion to reality.

III *Animals*

Most later critics considered landscape the pinnacle of Sung
painting, but the modern connoisseur cannot avoid a strong attrac-
tion to the incredible vitality of animal painting during this period.
We have already discussed the intimate relation between landscape
painting and poetry, so we will find it useful to examine animal
painting in China briefly before we explore Yang's animal poetry.
Although no paintings have been found so far from the Shang and
early Chou periods, we can form a rough idea about the painting
from the designs of the world famous bronze art of Shang and Chou
China. Even in this remote period of Chinese history, the artist was
much more interested in the representation of animal forms than
human. Some of the most recent archeological finds in China prove
that the brilliance of Chinese animal art remained undimmed into
Han times, but from about the fifth century B.C.,[75] the human form
increasingly dominated Chinese painting and sculpture and remained the center of interest until about the tenth century in both
secular and religious art. The great revolution in the tenth and
eleventh centuries, which led to the complete domination of landscape painting, affected the painting of animals, too, because al-

though the Sung painter was extremely adept at realistic portraits of human beings, paintings of animals outnumber those of men by a very great margin. Although Five Dynasties artists such as Huang Ch'üan (903–968) had already brought the art of animal painting to a high level, the Southern Sung period in which Yang lived was the golden age of realistic animal painting. The technical skill and psychological insight of these painters was never equaled again in China or any other part of the world.

No Western art critic has studied sufficiently the reasons why the Chinese were so much more interested in animals than men. During the Shang and early Chou periods, this interest may have been dictated by the various totemic religious cults of bronze age Chinese culture, and the rise of the human as the center of art in late Chou and Han times was most likely connected with the increasing influence of Confucian humanism, an idea which is reinforced by the didactic intent of much Han and Six Dynasties painting.[76]

In late Chou philosophy only the Taoists seem very sensitive toward animals, and Chuang-tzu (369–286 B.C.?) is obviously delighted by even lowly animals, as in his famous debate with Hui-shih (380–305 B.C.?) when he says: "The minnows come out and wander about completely at ease. This is the pleasure of fish."[77] Although Chuang-tzu uses his statement as the occasion for a debate with Hui Shih concerning problems of epistemology, the passage still shows a love of the animal world which the Taoists retained until much later times. Although the reverence for nature and her creatures by the Taoists had the greatest impact on the Chinese view of animal life, it is very likely that the Buddhist notion of transmigration played a very significant role. When this doctrine was first introduced to the Chinese in Han times, they found it quite difficult to accept, but after a few centuries, it was totally absorbed into the stream of Chinese religious beliefs and still plays an extremely important part in popular cults.[78] If a bird was once another human being in his past life, possibly even one's ancestor, it was much easier to see the animal as something different from a pet, item of food, or zoological specimen, as is usually the case in European art and literature.

However, in the earliest monument of Chinese poetry, the *Classic of Poetry*, animals largely serve as actors in the background of human life. The very first stanza of the first poem in the collection shows this tendency clearly:

> *Kuan, kuan,* cries the osprey
> On an island in the river.
> Lovely is the pure lady,
> A good match for a prince. [79]

Many of the animals of the *Classic of Poetry* are used allegorically, although the exact significance of the allegories is frequently lost to the modern reader. In fact, from the earliest times the allegorical use of animals in Chinese poetry has been very popular, and Tu Fu was working in a long established tradition when he wrote his well-known "Ballad of the Thin Horse":

> A thin horse in the eastern suburbs makes me sad,
> For his bones are hard and tough as a stone wall.
> If, hobbled, he tried to move, he would fall over flat;
> He certainly has no thought of prancing anymore.

After further description of the horse's pitiful condition, Tu Fu writes:

> Seeing men, you are dejected and seem to complain;
> Your master lost, you are depressed, lusterless.
> Weather cold, you are let roam far, geese your sole companions;
> In the evening, not taken in, crows peck at your sores.
> Who will care for you, so you can repay his favor?
> Then you can try again next year, when the spring
>   grass is tall. [80]

Although Tu Fu is very compassionate to the unfortunate horse, there is no doubt that his poem is a political allegory in which the horse represents the poet himself, who has been rejected by the court but would like to be given one more chance to prove himself despite his old age. It is important to note that the greatest horse painters of the T'ang dynasty such as Han Kan (d. 783?) were contemporaries of Tu Fu, and much of their horse painting, which was done in the imperial court, can be interpreted in a similar allegorical fashion. [81]

Yang Wan-li sometimes uses animals allegorically as did earlier poets and painters:

The Song of the Water Mantis[82]

In early morning I open the mat door to wash my face,
And a huge mantis races about on the water.
He sticks out two legs in front—like autumn bamboo poles;
Drags his belly behind—a spring fishing boat.
By chance he picks up a broken spider's web;
Grabs its four corners and sinks it in the deep abyss.
The mantis on the willow is good at catching locusts,
While the mantis on the water is trying to catch sturgeon.
If a mantis catches locusts, he can get one every meal,
But if he catches sturgeon, when can he get a sturgeon to eat?[83]

Although Yang's work shows an unusual degree of detailed observation of the water insect, the mantis is largely a vehicle for teaching a moral lesson. Yang is telling us that one should not attempt to be what one is not, and if one attempts to go beyond one's natural limits, one will suffer the same fate as the starving mantis.

In another poem Yang moves slightly away from the allegorical treatment of animals:

I Set off at Morning from Rush Field and am Moved When I See an Egret

I sigh because my whole life has been spent on the road;
I can't stand the mud and rain or driving my carriage on.
The egret is supposed to be the purest and loftiest of
us all,
But he's in the creek at the crack of dawn—so what's
his line?[84]

In earlier Chinese painting and poetry, egrets and cranes were symbols for purity and longevity, as Yang himself informs us. However, Yang's poem turns the old symbolism of the egret upside down, for he denies the total purity of the bird, since it must hunt for a living just as a worldly scholar-official such as himself.

Yang's poem has gone a long way in stripping away the human imposed mythology surrounding the egret, yet Yang is still projecting human values onto the animal world. In all cultures men have attempted to see animals organized in a pattern similar to human society, and Yang himself enjoyed the same practice:

Watching Ants
(First Poem of Two)

When by chance they meet one another, they carefully
    ask the way;
I wonder what the reason is they move home so many times.
How much do their tiny bodies need to feast upon?
One hunt, they return home, rearguard chariots filled![85]

Although Yang has described the ants as being subject to a society
similar to that of human beings, he does not attempt to draw any
moral about "industrious ants" as European authors would. His
reference to "rearguard chariots" is a piece of human fancy, but his
close observation of the way in which ants actually communicate
with each other while hunting food is completely new in Chinese
poetry.

Yang sees animals in a totally different light from T'ang authors,
for his attitude toward animals has much in common with his treatment of the landscape. The animals in Yang's poetry are commonly
as friendly as the mountains:

At Morning I Set Out From *Dharma* Enlightenment Monastery
    at Prayer Gate and Follow a Stream through a
        Dangerous, Inaccessible Area

The mountains lack people or smoke, the water, bridges;
The stream's vast, vast, the rain so desolate.
What good is it for this pair of egrets to comfort me?
As soon as they've passed by, I'll be even lonelier![86]

Mountains come down to welcome the weary traveler, and egrets
attempt to comfort the poet on his perilous voyage.

By suggesting the futility of his friendship with the egrets, Yang
hints that animals, too, are ultimately as unapproachable as the
mountains which hide themselves behind mist and clouds:

Cooking Breakfast at Jade Field, I Hear an Oriole and See a Stork
(First Poem of Two)

In the morning cold, he watches his reflection,
    admiring his golden robe;
He isn't willing to sing while I listen to him intently.

He flies into the willow shade where there are many hiding-places;
A few notes—he only lets the falling blossoms know.[87]

The oriole may delight us with his bright colors, but he is just as inaccessible as distant mountain peaks. Like the crags that hide in fog, he is engaging in the same "conspiracy of nature" against the human intellect.

We have already hinted at the novelty of Yang's careful observation of ant life, but in the next poem we find such observation stripped of any of the earlier allegorical elements:

The Raven

The children look at each other and just laugh at it;
Even this old fellow manages to grin a little.
A single raven flies and perches on the crooked railing's corner;
If you look closely, it really *does* have a beard![88]

Before the Sung dynasty, no Chinese poet would have looked at a raven so closely as to notice its whiskers, for he would probably be more interested in the raven as an inauspicious bird. Yang's examination of small details is quite consistent with his Ch'anist background, because Ch'an teaches the identity of everyday life and enlightenment. Yet, Yang's close observation of natural objects is closely related to non-Buddhist intellectual forces, which reached their peak during Yang's lifetime in the neo-Confucian philosophy of Chu Hsi. One of the most important doctrines of Chu Hsi's philosophy was *ko-wu*, or the "investigation of things," and although Chu normally directed his investigations to ethical and political matters, he also had a deep interest in natural phenomena, especially geology and cosmology.[89] Since Yang was a close friend of Chu Hsi, it would not be rash to speak of neo-Confucian influence on his animal poetry at least. However, it is not necessary to prove direct influence, for Chu Hsi's concept of *ko-wu* was an outgrowth of even wider tendencies in Chinese culture during the eleventh and twelfth centuries. The Sung love of detailed analysis gave rise to the golden age of Chinese science and mathematics just as it influenced the direction taken by Sung thinkers such as Chang Tsai, the Ch'eng brothers, and finally Chu Hsi himself. The analytical nature of much Sung culture led to detailed observation of landscape and animals in the painting of the period, for in painting we have the highly realistic animal paintings of the Southern Sung academy and in literature the animal poetry of Yang Wan-li and his contemporaries.

No one has seriously studied the effect of Ch'an Buddhism on these developments of Sung culture, but in an extremely perceptive passage the modern historian of Chinese thought, Feng Yu-lan, writes:

> Thus, the Ch'an school took a further step in synthesizing the sublime with the common. Yet if carrying water and chopping wood are really the nature of the mysterious *Tao*, why should it still be necessary for the man engaged in spiritual cultivation to abandon his family and become a monk? Why should not the mysterious *Tao* equally consist in performing the duties of father and sovereign? Here there was need for a further word, and it became the mission of the neo-Confucianists . . . to say that word.[90]

Consistent with the general tendencies of Sung culture, Yang carefully observes even the smallest creatures:

The Freezing Fly

> Through the window, by chance, I see a fly sunning himself;
> Rubbing two legs together, he plays in the morning sunlight.
> He knows beforehand the sun's rays are about to move;
> Suddenly he flies off, drops on another window—bzzzz.[91]

In contrast to earlier animal poems, the fly is now independent of the world of man, and Yang, the poet, is only an inactive bystander. Yang's description of the fly rubbing its legs together and his knowledge of the fly's search for sunlight prove that he had spent many long hours observing his subject, just as the neo-Confucian studied political history or the Southern Sung academic painter, birds.

Through his close observations of animals Yang achieved a comprehension of animals' feelings as profound as any human mind could possess, and rather than projecting human emotions into fish as earlier poets would have, he writes of fish as they exist in nature:

Watching Fish

> This old fellow can't stand the heat,
> So I sit barefooted on a tile drum bench.
> Near a pool, I watch the fish swimming;
> Focusing my eyes, I count them over and over.

> The minnows are especially afraid of people;
> They want to cross over but don't dare.
> One fish tries going on ahead
> To report if there are any special dangers.
> The school of fish at first wants to follow,
> But, wavering, they finally turn back.
> From time to time I pass the wine cup,
> As the day suddenly turns to dusk.[92]

Yang describes how he carefully focuses his eyes to count the fish over and over again. His habits of observation have much in common with modern scientific methods, but he is no cold statistician, for one can easily sense the joy in his depiction of the timid minnows' emotions.

Yang Wan-li was not just a master in the description of a single type of animal, but, like the Sung animal painters, he was able to capture the interreactions between animals:

I Write What I Saw in Jest

> The peasants do not send their children to herd pigs,
> For the old ravens play the pig-herder for them.
> Unashamed of this low post, they are actually elated;[93]
> Using stalks of grass, they play games with the pigs.
> One raven drives the pigs like cows herded to slaughter,
> While another rides a pig like the Queen Mother's steed.[94]
> When their ride isn't steady or the ravens can't drive them on,
> They sit and watch the stubborn pigs, for no whip's at hand.
> Though men are different from horses or cows,
> All of us spend our whole lives in Raven Robe Alley.[95]
> Scolding the pigs, the ravens caw till their beaks are parched,
> But in the end the pigs don't understand a word of raven talk.
> The riding raven doesn't follow, so herder raven fights him;
> They fight over cows, argue about horses, no bystanders to help.
> The pigs merely continue eating and walking on their own;
> Letting the two ravens fight it out by themselves.
> Unexpectedly, a young boy drives the ravens away,
> And within a second, they are fighting to the death![96]

Although no painting on exactly the same subject survives from the Sung dynasty, the Sung painters similarly enjoyed showing the play of emotions between animals. In one well-known painting attributed to Ts'ui Po (fl. 1068–1077) in the Taiwan Palace Museum, two

jays scold a hare which has accidentally wandered into their territory, while the hare looks back at them with an expression of puz-
zled amusement.[97] Just as in most of Yang's animal poems, the
animals of the painting live separate from the human world, as they
could be observed in their natural habitat.

IV *Plants*

Plants have played a role in Chinese art and literature as important as animals, and, as one would expect from our discussion of
animals, the realistic portrayal of plants in paintings and their detailed description in poetry reached its climax in Southern Sung
times. Just as in his animal poetry, Yang usually avoids the earlier
largely allegorical use of plants in Chinese verse:

> I Sing of a Bamboo Grove in Front of the Water Pavilion
> by Ch'iang-t'ien at Ten Mile Pool

> As soon as I see this gentleman's face,[98]
> The barren village is no longer merely a village.
> Under slanting sunlight, he's a Wen T'ung original;[99]
> The sparrow roosting on him must be Wang Hui-chih's soul.
> Alas! I can do nothing about my wanderer's longings,
> But at least we can talk together about my poetic sorrow.
> I ask him: "Would you like a drink?"
> Then pour some wine on his frosty roots.[100]

In this poem past and present reverence for the bamboo is combined, for Wang Hui-chih was a man of the third century, while
Wen T'ung was a typical Sung intellectual who was famed for both
his painting and poetry and lived only a short two generations before
Yang Wan-li. Yang is certainly very conscious of past traditions concerning the bamboo in the poem, but he does not regard the bamboo merely as a symbol of rectitude as many a pre-Sung author
would have. Instead, the bamboo is a hearty drinking companion.
   This form of close personal relationship between poet and plant is
exactly the same as we have observed between poet and landscape:

> Written on the Wang Family Inn at Green Mountain Market

> The small building overlooks a short wall;
> Half a trellis of long spring flowers pulses with
> florid fragrance.

The sunny flowers know that I am lonely,
For they fly to me on purpose, entering my bamboo window.[101]

This close identity with the creatures of nature causes Yang to sympathize with flowers even after they have fallen from their trees:

The Day after the *Shang-ssu* Festival I Stroll in the
East Garden Again with Tzu-wen, Po-chuang, and Yung-nien

We penetrate the nine paths full of shade, one by one;
Talking and laughing, each of us is delighted.
We walk slowly, but not because we lack strength;
We can't bear advancing on the fallen blossoms covering
        the ground.[102]

Yang's sympathy for plants is a trait he held in common with even earlier Sung poets, and Huang T'ing-chien, Yang's model during his youth, wrote:

On the Subject of Herding Oxen in my Bamboo and Rocks

In my fields is a little knoll,
With a dark bamboo grove, luxuriantly green.
A herding boy holding a three-foot whip
Drives along his old, trembling oxen.
I love my rocks very much,
So don't let your oxen sharpen horns on them.
If they sharpen their horns, it's still all right,
But if the oxen fight, they'll break my bamboos![103]

Huang T'ing-chien feels strongly about his bamboos, but one wonders if he is more concerned for his private property than for the plants. In any case, he does not consider the bamboos to exist on a plane similar to human life, as Yang Wan-li so often does.

Yang's sympathy for plants enables him to understand the "emotions" of the vegetable world and ascribe human feelings to its denizens:

In the Evening Heat I Roam by a Lotus Pond
(Third Poem of Five)

The fine grasses shake their heads and announce him to me,
So I open my robe and stop the whole west wind.

The lotus enter evening, yet still worry about the heat,
So they lower their faces, hiding themselves, deep in
    their azure umbrellas.[104]

Yang interprets the natural movement of the grasses in the wind as
an announcement to him that the west wind of autumn is coming to
relieve him from the summer heat. Since the poet himself is suffering from the torrid weather, he imagines the lotuses are hiding in
fear of the heat.

Since plants possess human emotions, Yang can write about his
favorite flower, the plum, as if it were a real human being:

Picking a Plum with Snow under Candlelight

Brother Plum dashes through the snow to visit me;
Snow flakes cover his beard and even his face.[105]
All his life, Plum's been skinny but now he's fat;
Is it because I can't distinguish Plum and the snow?
I call him in and look him over by lamplight;
Now I really don't know if there's any snow or not.
All I see is his jade countenance wet with beads of sweat;
The sweat covers his face and drips down to his beard![106]

The detailed description of the plum flower is worthy of Sung painters who specialized in painting plum flowers, but the most striking
feature of the poem is Yang's highly original use of personification of
plant life, a device not very common even by Northern Sung times.

Attributing human qualities to plants presents Yang with the
same "conspiracy of nature" we have noticed in his depiction of the
landscape and animal kingdom:

Two blossoms, three branches, the plums are just new;
Neither thin nor thick, they're at their height.
Flowering branches line the path and scold me as I pass;
Catching my cap, they snatch it from my old man's head![107]

The flowers may put on a beautiful show for men, but they still
enjoy playing tricks on humans in the same way mountains and birds
do.

The Western reader may find it quite difficult to comprehend
how the Chinese poet managed to conceive of plants in such human
terms, but even today Chinese ascribe different personalities to

plants and may even use plants to describe the personalities of humans. Thus, the peony is flamboyant and sensuous, while the plum is refined and chaste, and the two flowers can be used to describe two corresponding types of women. The Taoist idea of living in harmony with nature must have been a major factor in such a view of plants, but just as the Buddhist doctrine of transmigration played a large role in the Chinese sympathy for animals, so it must have functioned with regard to plants. Although the Indian Buddhists do not mention reincarnation in plants, the concept of an underlying Buddha nature behind all creation, animate and inanimate, became so well developed that the common folk believed in a host of flower fairies, and one nineteenth-century novel, *Ching Hua Yüan* (literally, *Karmic Affinities of Flowers in the Mirror*), is concerned with the transmigration of flower spirits.[108] This belief in a "soul" in plants may partially explain the different personalities one senses in Sung flower paintings and the personification of plants in Yang Wan-li's poetry.

CHAPTER 7

The Transcendence of Sorrow

THE great modern Japanese scholar of Chinese literature, Yoshikawa Kōjirō, wrote that one of the most distinctive characteristics of Sung poetry lies in the poets' "transcendence of sorrow."[1] With few exceptions Chinese poetry before the Sung dynasty was dominated by a feeling of intense melancholy, which was relieved in the case of only a few extraordinary authors such as Han Yü or Po Chü-yi. Early Sung poets such as Ou-yang Hsiu and Mei Yao-ch'en, who broke away from older poetic traditions, were among the first Chinese writers to reject this pessimistic mood, and, in general, the Northern Sung authors wrote poetry distinguished by an optimism unparalleled in earlier Chinese literature. This optimism reached its height in the works of the greatest Northern Sung poet, Su Shih.

However, toward the end of the Northern Sung period, the Kiangsi poets, and Huang T'ing-chien, in particular, revived T'ang seriousness to a certain degree, and in his earlier works imitative of the Kiangsi masters, Yang Wan-li was influenced by their example:

Night Rain

This secluded man sleeps so soundly
He doesn't know the river rains have come.
A frightful wind rises with a moan;
It sounds like mountain peaks splitting.
I sit up, no longer able to sleep,
And a myriad feelings gather in my old breast.
I recall that when I was fourteen or fifteen
I read books in our study under the pines.
Now, in a cold night, distressed, I await dawn;
Chanting alone, still, without companions.
Insects chatter, my single lamp silent;

> Ghosts shriek, the myriad mountains mourn.
> The sound of rain has always been thus;
> Though it drips on my stout heart, I'll not despair.
> Now I've passed the age of fifty;[2]
> Ten years earlier I was already in decay.
> I don't know what will come afterwards;
> Will my stout heart ever return?
> My old studies more distant and fruitless daily;
> My books turned to dust long ago.
> The state of sagehood seems far off as heaven,
> And my old age oppresses me sorely.
> As I sit thinking, my melancholy is endless,
> Yet at my east window, the dawn's light unfolds.[3]

There are many elements in Yang's poem which remind us of T'ang dynasty and earlier verse, such as references to the moaning wind, chirping insects, and approaching old age and death. When he adds shrieking ghosts to the list, we might even feel we are reading one of Li Ho's milder works, although Yang's ghosts are not real and are only a description of the wind's melancholy sound.

Yang may mourn his studies falling behind and his distance from the state of sagehood, but he sounds a more positive note than most T'ang writers when he says: "Though it drips on my stout heart, I'll not despair." The typical T'ang poem on old age would end with apes crying mournfully in the distant forest, or the poet rinsing his handkerchief with hot tears, but Yang chooses to conclude on the more optimistic note of the approaching sunrise. It is quite likely that the ending of his poem was influenced by the conclusion Su Shih gave to the first part of his famous prose-poem "Red Cliff." After discussing the sadness of time's passing and the impermanence of human life, Su Shih manages to transcend these sorrows which had troubled generations of Chinese scholars, finishing his poem in the following manner:

> The meats and fruits finished, the cups and bowls
> in confusion, we lay down, leaning against each other
> in the bottom of the boat, not knowing that the east
> is already growing light.[4]

As with Yang, the sunrise is a symbol for the renewed hope of life. Even before his poetical enlightenment, Yang had begun transcending the youthful pessimism still remaining in the previous poem:

Watching the Rain

Clouds rise from the top of Grace Mountain
And hurl their rain at the foot of Great Lake.
At first I worried as I watched them afar;
Now suddenly rain is falling on top my head.
White feathers of rain veil my raven cloth cap;
And my robe sleeves are already soaking wet.
I come home and see the eaves' torrents,
Seeming to drain ten-thousand-yard deep chasms.
The thunder cracks, like a huge jade pot;
Lightning flashes, a wet silver rope.
In a moment the water is level with my stairs;
The flowered bank loses half of one corner.
I know for sure the rice paddies are full
And can clearly imagine the old peasants' joy.
Recently, during the change from spring to summer,
The drought has been much too cruel.
Having raced all over mountains and rivers,
The clouds now lie scattered and desolate.
My two temples had grown white through worry,
And my knees were bruised from kneeling in prayer.
All along I knew it was going to rain today,
So my old breast was fussing about nothing![5]

We constantly discover Yang Wan-li chiding himself for worrying too much about problems for which he can offer no solution, such as the drought confronting him in this poem. It must be stressed that Yang's attitude is not similar to the fatalism of many earlier Chinese authors, for Yang possessed a genuinely optimistic outlook on life, which enabled him to encounter any sorrow with good humor. As a result, Yang rarely engages in self-pity in his later verse, reserving, instead, his compassion for others less fortunate than himself. Thus, he does not worry that he has just been drenched by the rainstorm or that water is flooding his land, for he is overjoyed that the peasants have been spared from a devastating drought.

One of the most irritating features of some pre-Sung Chinese poets is the tendency to complain about the most trivial of difficulties. Su Shih himself greatly disliked this weakness of Chinese *literati*, and reserves some of his strongest invective for poets such as Meng Chiao, who could find nothing good to say about life.[6] Weakness was not restricted to pre-Sung scholars, however, and one day when Su was walking outside with some friends, it started to rain. When his friends scurried to find a hiding place, Su walked merrily on, and chided them with the following *tz'u* poem:

To the Tune of "Settling the Wind and Waves"

Don't listen to the rain's sound piercing groves
 and beating leaves;
What's the matter with walking slowly and singing?
A bamboo staff and grass shoes are lighter than a horse.
Who's afraid?
We pass our whole life in a downpour of mist and rain![7]

Like Su, Yang refused to become worried by all of the little problems of life:

In the Morning I Leave the Prefectural City to Go to
Chih-hsia and Visit Hu Tuan-ming, Riding a Boat
Back at Night[8]

From the prefectural city to Chih-hsia
Is not an easy journey in even two days.
I do not desire to race about this way,
But an imperial order compels me to southern travels.[9]
When I leave the city, the stars have not set yet,
But when I return, the moon is already out.
I ask how deep the water is,
But the boatmen chatter on without reply.
Soon the rocks in the water answer for them:
Whoosh! The roar of tumbling rapids.
Perilous peaks loom in the evening, blue;
Hidden pools arise in the night, pure.
The river turns, and the wind comes moaning;
It's hard to conceal the nobs of my sickly shoulders.
At first too lazy to hunt for more clothes,
I finally just can't stand the cold.
As we come within one or two miles of the city,
On the far shore—three or four lamps.
I gaze at the gate, afraid they've closed up early;
Though I urge the boat on, we move only slowly.

How kind is the half ring of a moon!
A long time she's been inclining westward.
About to set, she waits a little longer,
For she knows I want to enter the city.
The moon is delicate and her rays but few,
So the big stars help her out with their light.
I have reached home, but my heart's not yet calmed,
From the watchtower, it's only eight o'clock![10]

Yang is in a hurry because of pressing official business, but he is
delayed by adverse traveling conditions and suffers from hunger and
cold. Still, the world is basically kind to him, for the moon helps him
in his journey home, enabling him to arrive back much earlier than
he had expected. As usual, his worries were needless.

Despite the many political setbacks he suffered, Yang Wan-li believed that most things turn out well in the end and that the pessimism of earlier poets was baseless:

Entering the Boundary of Floating Beam

The wet sun pales midst clouds;
Clear peaks freshen after rain.
Water swallows the dike willow's knees;
Wheat reaches country boys' shoulders.
Whirlpools play with floating leaves;
Cooking smoke enters our boat backward.[11]
The current is with us and so is the wind,
Though people say you can't get *two* good things at once![12]

Although Yang is making fun of pessimists during his own age, he
obviously has pessimists of earlier times in mind, too. The popular
saying which he quotes in the last line of the poem was ancient by
Yang's time and reflected the gloomy mood of T'ang and earlier
periods.

Only a detailed study of Sung society would tell us the reasons for
the Sung scholar's optimism, but it would be proper to hazard a few
guesses here. First of all, the Sung period was probably the most
politically enlightened which China had yet seen. Although the
political situation regarding the barbarians was no cause for optimism, even in Northern Sung times, the internal political climate
was not as full of violence and terror as earlier periods, for the Sung

emperors rarely engaged in the brutal executions of officials who lost favor, as in earlier times. Even during the heated debate between conservatives and reformers in the time of Wang An-shih, the defeated party was not summarily beheaded but merely removed from office, and at the worst, exiled to South China. Men in opposite political camps, such as Wang An-shih and Su Shih, could remain on good terms throughout their lives.

One further political reason for the optimism of the Sung intellectual was the much greater social mobility achieved through the civil service examinations. Although the examinations had become effective in the T'ang dynasty, the majority of men passing the examinations came from families of aristocratic background in which they were exposed to the kind of education necessary for success. But with the widespread use of printing by the eleventh century, literacy became much commoner and education was available to many more people than before. Such men of humble backgrounds as Yang Wan-li had a better chance of succeeding in the political system of the Sung.

Greater social mobility is closely connected to an improvement in economic conditions, and the economic expansion of Sung China was probably a major impetus to a more optimistic outlook on life. In the eleventh and twelfth centuries China went through a tremendous economic growth which greatly improved the living standard and created a larger middle class than had existed before. There was an unprecedented expansion of domestic and foreign trade, which led to the growth of a huge urban population separated from the conservatism of the countryside and less dependent on the whims of nature for a livelihood.[13] This increase of prosperity was accompanied by a lengthening of the life span, which was certainly helped by better sanitation through the drinking of tea, widespread use of porcelain dishes, and improved medical knowledge. Most of the great Sung poets lived to be old men, and Yang Wan-li himself died at the age of eighty. There is no question that the Sung intellectual had more to be optimistic about than earlier intellectuals, and the effect of their optimism can be seen in all aspects of Sung culture, including poetry.

As a result of his own optimism, Yang Wan-li treated many of the older themes of Chinese poetry in a very different way from T'ang authors. One of the greatest causes of anguish to the T'ang poet was the hardship of travel, frequently seen as an allegory for the difficulties encountered during the "voyage of life." Tu Fu wrote the following poem during one of his interminable voyages:

Ballad at the Ends of the World

An old man at the ends of the world, I cannot go home yet;
As evening comes I face the great river to the east, crying.
In Lung-yu, at the source of the Yellow River, fields
     lie untilled;[14]
Barbarian cavalry and soldiers enter our Pa and Shu.[15]
Huge waves swamp heaven, the wind tears up trees;
In front flies a bald crane, followed by a yellow goose.
Nine times I have sent my letters to Lo-yang,
But for ten years I have had no news of my family.[16]

Yang Wan-li himself traveled as much or even more than Tu Fu, but Yang's attitude toward this activity is much closer to the modern globe-trotting tourist:

Riding a River Boat Outside Heaven Gate
(First Poem of Five)

A new boat near the river village tests the water
     the first time,
So they start advertising for passengers and just
     happen on me.
Its single-beam board hut has just passed through the rain,
And oiled windows on both sides are good for reading books.
They've bought up all the peony flowers under the spring wind
And stuck them carelessly in the yew table and bamboo mats.
Midst these fragrant heaps it seems we're riding on
     a pine pavilion;
To enjoy all the thousands of mountains, who needs a
     donkey?[17]

Similar to the modern tourist, Yang pays more attention to details than Tu Fu, and the reader senses that Yang's journey is more concrete than Tu Fu's rather abstract travels, which, as we have said, are probably meant to be symbolic of his troubled life. But the most startling difference between the two poets is that Yang takes a positive delight in his travels, reading books and enjoying the scenery, while Tu Fu is in a total state of depression.

Su Shih summarized the new attitude in two short lines: "I was originally homeless, so where else can I go?/ My native village doesn't have such beautiful scenery!"[18] Although the Sung poet was still deeply attached to his native village, he was now willing to travel about in the larger world around him without the constant fear and anxiety that troubled earlier Chinese poets.

Another theme which earlier poets commonly used to express their pessimism was the description of the melancholy autumn season. Autumn was the time when plants die and animals migrate from their summer homes, and earlier Chinese poets felt autumn symbolized the constant change of the world and the brevity of human existence. The T'ang poet Meng Chiao's attitude toward the season is typical:

Autumn Thoughts
(Second Poem of Fifteen)

The face of the autumn moon freezes;
An old traveler, my will is exhausted.
The chill dew drips my dreams to pieces;
The harsh wind combs my bones, cold.
On my mat, the print of a sickly visage;
In my intestines, twisting sorrows writhe.
My thoughts doubtful, nothing reliable;
I listen emptily, completely without reason.
The *wu-t'ung* tree, wilted, looms above me;
It sounds and resounds like a sadly plucked string.[19]

Yang Wan-li agrees with Meng that the season is depressing, but he refuses to be overwhelmed in sorrow:

Moved by Autumn
(Third Poem of Six)

Failing light hurries on the night's gloom,
While my solitary lamp opens some evening brightness.
This old fellow is tired and would like to sleep;
I seem drunk yet wide awake, too.
My inch-long heart hasn't even an inch of regret,
For it is level as a river or the sea, so pure.
Then what are these autumn crickets doing
With their cry of resentment all about me?

Miserable, pitiful, it doesn't stop;
Rising, then falling, never at peace.
Whisper, whisper, a hundred thousand voices;
On and on, to the third and fourth watches.
I circle the steps but can't find them;
I sit still, but they resume their chirping contest.
You have mouths; go complain to yourselves:
But I'm drunk, so I won't listen to you![20]

Yang clearly contrasts his unfailing optimism, which does not feel
"even an inch of regret," with the mournful surroundings of the
autumn season. The autumn cricket which arouses sad feelings was a
faded cliché even by T'ang times, and Yang shows a wicked relish in
demolishing the stale imagery associated with the insect in earlier
times. Despite the attempt of these crickets to make him sad, his
optimism protects him from their sad cry.

Autumn was a symbol for old age and death among the Chinese,
and the fear of old age is one of the most overworked themes of
Chinese poetry, appearing already in the *Classic of Poetry.* Since
most Chinese intellectuals were skeptical about the chances of an
afterlife, death was particularly frightening to them, and at the first
appearance of white hairs, they were usually plunged into deep
sorrow. Such an attitude could lead to the *carpe diem* philosophy of
Li Po or to the quiet resignation to one's fate expressed in much of
T'ao Ch'ien's verse. We have already seen that Yang became increasingly tranquil as he approached old age, but his tranquility did
not arise from any fatalism but from a genuine joy for life in all its
aspects:

Riding a River Boat Outside Heaven Gate
(Second Poem of Five)

Soon as I get on the boat, I chance to face a mountain,
And in one moment the mountain changes so many ways.
At first it piles up its kingfisher covers into
    thousands of folds;
Suddenly it unsheathes it blue jade into two or
    three canes.
The children on both shores seem to be standing in heaven;
Towers and pavilions of several villages flash by.
In all my life when did I ever dream of so much fun?
Shooting the rapids at Heaven Gate when I'm old![21]

Yang was already into his seventies when he wrote this poem, an age
when most T'ang poets were long dead. Yet instead of indulging in
whining self-pity, Yang expresses an unbounded joy in the experiences of each moment.

All of Yang's later poetry is suffused with an ecstasy for man's life
unmatched by even the Northern Sung poets:

I Wash My Face, a Short Poem

> On both shores, the Che Mountains send off my
>   returning boat,
> Freshly beaten spring indigo dyes them a light blue.
> I draw up the river's waves to wash and rinse my mouth;
> In the pure morning, my face is fragrant as falling blossoms![22]

Yang can celebrate such a simple joy as washing his face in the
morning.

Although social conditions played an important role in forming his
personality, Yang's training in Ch'an Buddhism with its emphasis on
everyday life obviously was very important in allowing him to transcend sorrow and find pleasure in the commonest occurrences. Yet
the greatest solace for Yang and other Sung poets was the contemplation of the beauties of nature, the source of all the mysteries
which the Ch'an monk or Taoist recluse strove to understand:

Moved by Autumn
(Fifth Poem of Six)

> On fall mornings one can still stand the cold,
> But the fall nights are so hard to pass.
> The dark lamp shines on my volumes of books,
> And both my eyes seem to be in a fog.
> I close my books and sit up alone;
> All by myself, with whom can I talk?
> I try to lie down, but can't stand lying;
> I get up to walk, but there's no place to go.
> Suddenly there's a light in the corner of my room;
> The mountain moon has come to my garden door.
> She seems to pity this secluded, old man;
> In the depth of night she engages me in pure conversation.
> I chant and the moon knows how to listen;[23]
> The moon turns, and I follow her along.
> Why do I have to read any more books?
> I'll just write verses together with the moon![24]

In the end, books are of no use to Yang, for they merely becloud the
eyes and the intellect. Friendship with other men is also of limited
value, for Yang is alone with no one to talk to him. Eventually it is
the moon which brings comfort to Yang, and he feels a unity with
her that transcends the normal relationships between friends. When
he writes "I chant and the moon knows how to listen," he is pur-
posely making fun of the feeling of isolation which Li Po and other
poets felt throughout their lives. Yang had been enlightened to the
unity behind all the universe.

CHAPTER 8

Posterity

WITH the beginning of the Ming dynasty, Yang Wan-li's poetry and Sung poetry in general gradually fell into disrepute. Whatever comments we do find about Yang are usually negative, for Chinese poetry came under the thrall of the Former Seven Masters (Ch'ien-ch'i-tzu) and Latter Seven Masters (Hou-ch'i-tzu) who considered imitation of the T'ang poets to be the highest form of poetic writing. When the attack against the conservatives came, it was led by Yüan Hung-tao (1568–1610) of the Kung-an School, which had been strongly influenced by the thought of the more radical members of Wang Shou-jen's (1472–1579) neo-Confucian School of the Mind, especially the notorious Li Chih.[1] We have already seen how Ch'an Buddhism led Yang Wan-li to oppose literary conservatism, and in this connection it is important to mention that the more radical disciples of Wang Shou-jen learned so much from Ch'an that orthodox Confucians derisively labeled them Wildcat Ch'an (Yeh-hu-ch'an).

Although Yüan Hung-tao does not discuss Yang Wan-li's verse, his opposition to imitation and sterile conventions is quite similar to Yang's position:

Upon reaching the modern age, poetry and prose have become extremely inferior. People claim one must take the Ch'in and Han dynasties as one's standard for prose and the flourishing T'ang as the standard for poetry. Pilfering and plagiarizing, imitating and copying, they follow the ancients like a shadow or echo. If people see someone with even one word that is not imitative, they band together and accuse him of belonging to the wildcat heterodox path. People did not formerly know that prose should take Ch'in and Han as its standard, for when did the Ch'in and Han authors ever imitate the Six Confucian Classics word for word? As for poetry taking the flourishing T'ang as its standard, when did the poets of the flourishing T'ang ever imitate those of the Han and Wei dynasties word for word? If the Ch'in

147

and Han had imitated the Six Classics, then how could the prose of the Ch'in and Han ever have come into being? If the flourishing T'ang had imitated Han and Wei, how would there ever have been poetry of the flourishing T'ang?[2]

Although it is nearly impossible to prove any direct influence of Yang Wan-li on Yüan Hung-tao, they were both members of a common stream of Chinese thought deeply indebted to the Ch'an stress upon individualism and spontaneity.

In fact, it was precisely Yang Wan-li's opposition to formalism and his advocation of self-expression that had the greatest influence on later poetic theory and practice, as can be seen in the case of Yüan Mei (1716–1797), one of the most original poets in Chinese literature and a leading critic of the eighteenth century. By Ch'ing times, Sung poetry had been rehabilitated, and by the eighteenth and nineteenth centuries, the flood of anti-traditional writers were able to appreciate Yang Wan-li's individualistic qualities better. In his critical work *Poetry Talks of Sui-yüan*, Yüan Mei ascribes the following saying to Yang Wan-li:

Yang Wan-li said: "Why is it that people of low natural abilities love to speak of meter and tonal patterns but do not understand style and interest? Meter and tonal patterns are an empty scaffolding with a 'tune' one can easily imitate. Style and interest alone express the natural genius *(hsing-ling)* and only a talented poet can accomplish this." I deeply love Yang's words.[3]

The quotation does not survive in Yang Wan-li's works, but it certainly conforms to his basic ideas on literature. Anyone who is familiar with Yüan Mei's poetry can easily find strong resemblances to Yang Wan-li's verse in Yüan's daring individualism and extensive use of humor. These similarities must have struck one of Yüan's students, for Yüan writes:

Wang Ta-shen said that my poems are similar to Yang Wan-li's, but Fan Shou-sheng disagreed with him violently and came to tell me. I was startled by this and replied: "Yang Wan-li is the master of his age, so how could I easily resemble him? Later people disliked his poetry for its 'carving and engraving' and frequently made light of Yang, for they did not know that his natural talent was pure and miraculous, extremely similar to Li Po. He did not cover up his faults with his virtues, which was precisely his sincerest point. As for his moral courage and his writings, these are all preseved in his biography, and even if I wanted to imitate him, I would be too shy of myself!"[4]

Despite Yüan Mei's modesty in thinking himself unworthy to imitate Yang Wan-li, Yang's influence is evident in many of his poems and Yüan's theory of *hsing-ling,* or "natural genius," in poetry is basically identical to Yang Wan-li's conception of enlightenment as the key to the writing of original poetry.

Notes and References

References to the page numbers of Yang Wan-li's poems are as follows. The first number refers to the *chüan* and page numbers in the *Ssu-pu ts'ung-k'an* (abbreviated *SPTK*) edition of the *Ch'eng-chai chi* (abbreviated *CCC*). The second number is that of the *chüan* and page in the *Ssu-pu pei-yao* edition. If a third number appears, it is the page number of the poem in Chou Ju-ch'ang's *Yang Wan-li hsüan-chi* (abbreviated *YWLHC*). Generally speaking, the readings of *SPTK* have been followed, and whenever I disagree with *SPTK*, this has been noted.

Chapter One

1. Other than the poetic and prose works, the main source for Yang Wan-li's life is his biography contained in *Sung-shih, chüan* 433. Also useful is a *nien-p'u* in Hsia Ching-kuan, *Yang Ch'eng-chai shih hsüan chu, Wan-yu wen-k'u hui-yao*, no. 0908 (reprint, Taipei, 1965). Another *nien-p'u* in Hu Ming-t'ing, "Yang Wan-li shih p'ing-shu," *Ta-lu tsa-chih, chüan* 9, nos. 7–8, pp. 51–60, contains some valuable information. Chou Ju-ch'ang's footnotes to Yang's autobiographical poems also contain a wealth of information.
2. See I. Y. Lo, *Hsin Chi'i-chi* (New York: Twayne Publishers, 1971). Hsin's youth is dealt with on pp. 22–25.
3. *Lu Yu, Lu Fang-weng ch'üan-chi* (abbreviated *LFWCC*) *SPPY*, 65–6a.
4. For all official titles I have depended on E. A. Kracke, *Translation of Sung Civil Service Titles* (Paris, 1957).
5. *Sung-shih* (abbreviated *SS*), K'ai-ming shu-chü, 5594–c.
6. *CCC*, 81–676b.
7. Yang describes his burning of the earlier poems in a preface to his earliest collection. See *CCC*, 80–672a.
8. 2–18b; 2–6a.
9. The "short lamp" is one used by a poor scholar who has not yet obtained high position.
10. Allusion to Feng Hsüan of the Warring States Period who served under Meng Ch'ang Chün of the state of Ch'i. When he first became a

retainer of Ch'i, he was not highly valued and played on his long sword while singing that he wished to return home because he had no fish to eat.

11. Reference to the Han poet Ssu-ma Hsiang-ju's famous work "Tzu-hsü fu" or "Prose-poem of Master Fiction." The work is narrated by the fanciful character Master Fiction and describes the wonders of the imperial hunting park in extravagant language. Yang suggests that only such unrealistic writing is appreciated by the present government. (4–38b; 4–5a; 49.)

12. 4–39a; 4–6a.

13. 4–39b; 4–6b.

14. 4–43b; 4–10a.

15. Yang is complaining about the excessive paperwork. Ancient government documents were written in red and black ink.

16. Yang is so occupied by official duties that he cannot write lines as famous as Wang Po's "In the evening, pearl curtains are rolled up midst West Mountain rain." See *SPTK*, Wang Po, *Wang Tzu-an chi*, 2–31b.

17. 6–55b; 6–5b; 57.

18. *CCC*, 89–770.

19. The Lin Bandits were peasant rebels who revolted in 1165 in Hunan province. The equal grain purchase was a government program which bought grain from the peasants to feed military and civil personnel. Frequently local officials did not pay the peasants for their grain.

20. Equal buying was similar to equal purchase but involved silk instead.

21. A silk tax supposedly levied to buy uniforms for the army stationed on the Huai River boundary with the Chin.

22. Ibid., 89–771.

23. Yang's study is named after the last line in a poem by the T'ang author Liu Tsung-yüan (733–819): "I fish alone in the cold river's snow." See Liu Tsung-yüan, *Chu-shih yin-pien T'ang Liu hsien-sheng chi, SPTK*, 43–218a.

24. Literally, "dream soul." (7–66a; 7–8b; 63).

25. 7–72b; 8–6b.

26. Forgetting words was an ideal of both Taoists and Buddhists.

27. One of the basic tenets of Ch'an is that enlightenment is nothing special or secret. See p. 48.

28. 7–69b; 8–3b. I follow the *SPPY* reading in the last line.

29. *CCC*, 80–672.

30. 8–80b; 9–6a.

31. 9–88a; 10–6a. I follow *SPPY* in line two.

32. The story of Vimalakīrti is contained in the *Vimala-kīrti-nirdeśa-sūtra*, or *Wei-mo-chieh suo-shuo ching* in Chinese. It is translated into French in E. Lamotte, *L'enseignement de Vimalakīrti* (Louvain, 1962).

33. 11–103b; 12–3b.

34. The green robe is the color of the unripe lichee. The fruit suddenly turns from green to bright red.

35. The lichee seems to have a cooling effect when one eats it in a tropical climate.

36. 15–143a; 16–7a.

37. The two immortals are probably Yang's contemporaries Yu Mou and Lu Yu.

38. 25–236b; 27–10a.

39. The Chin Tartars found it difficult to cross the river when invading south China. Wu is the area around modern Shanghai.

40. Yao-han is the famous Han-ku Pass in modern Honan province, a highly strategic area.

41. 27–255a; 29–4a; 170.

42. Both men were prime ministers in 1135 during the reign of Kao Tsung, but they were removed after Ch'in Kuei came to power.

43. 27–257a; 29–5b; 175.

44. Chang Tuan-yi, *Kuei-erh chi,* in *Ts'ung-shu chi-ch'eng* (Shanghai: Commercial Press, 1937), 45–a.

45. 38–358b; 39–1a.

46. T'ao Ch'ien (365–427) and Hsieh Ling-yün (385–433) were the two most famous poets of the North-south Period. They especially appealed to Yang because they were the founders of nature poetry in China.

47. 42–402b; 42–8b; 241.

48. 38–359b; 39–2b.

49. 42–400b; 42–6b.

50. Ibid.

51. *Taishō Shinshū Daizōkyō* (abbreviated *Taisho),* *Wei-mo-chieh suo-shuo ching,* no. 475, vol. 14, p. 551–c.

52. *SS,* 5595b.

53. Lo Ta-ching, *Ho-lin Yü-lu,* in *Pi-chi hsiao-shuo ta-kuan hsü-pien* (Taipei: Hsin-hsing shu-chü, 1962), *chüan* 4, p. 5, p. 2294a.

54. 38–360a; 39–2b.

Chapter Two

1. *SPTK,* Su Shih, *Chi-chu fen-lei Tung-p'o hsien-sheng shih* (abbreviated *TPHSS),* 21, 391–a.

2. Ibid., 18, 337–b.

3. Han Chü, *Ling-yang hsien-sheng shih,* Yao-tai shen-shih edition, 1910, 1, 8–b.

4. Wei Ch'ing-chih, *Shih-jen yü-hsieh* (Shanghai: Chung-hua shu-chü, 1959), 5, 122.

5. Kuo Shao-yü, *Chung-kuo wen-hsüeh p'i-p'ing shih,* p. 214.

6. *Shih-jen yü-hsieh,* 1, 8.

7. *CCC,* 80–672.

8. *Taisho, Ching-te ch'uan-teng lu* (abbreviated *CTCTL),* no. 2076, vol. 51, p. 264–b.

9. Ibid., p. 356–b.

10. "The pool has grass" is an allusion to Hsieh Ling-yün's famous line "The pool bears spring grasses" in his poem *"Teng ch'ih-shang lou."* See Ting Fu-pao, ed., *Ch'üan Han San-kuo Chin Nan-pei Ch'ao shih* (Taipei: Shih-chieh shu-chü reprint, 1962), vol. 2, p. 638.

11. "Eyes all in disorder" is from *Chuang-tzu*, "P'ien Mu": "The humane men of this age worry about the troubles of the world with eyes in disorder." See *SPTK, Nan-hua chen-ching*, 4, 69–a. Since there is considerable controversy about the meaning of this passage in *Chuang-tzu*, Yang's line is difficult to interpret. Chou Ju-ch'ang suggests that Yang means that the poet should concern himself with the practical problems of the world. In light of the mysticism apparent in both poems, I find Chou's interpretation difficult to accept, and so I suspect Yang means that the poet is unconscious of anything beyond his own poetry.

12. "When a monk asked, 'What was the meaning of Bodhidharma's coming from the West,' the master replied, 'A cedar in front of the courtyard.' " See *Taisho, Wu-men kuan* (abbreviated *WMK*), no. 2005, vol. 48, p. 297–b.

13. Reference to the Ch'an master Chih-ch'in, who was enlightened upon seeing a peach flower. Chou Ju-ch'ang states this story is from the *Shen-hsien chuan*, but I have not been able to locate the story.

14. 4–34b; 4–1a; 42

15. *CCC*, 80–672b.

16. 29–273a; 31–4a; 182.

17. See P. B. Yampolsky, *The Platform Sutra of the Sixth Patriarch* (New York: Columbia University Press), p. 172.

18. *WMK*, 293–b.

19. *SPTK, Yü-chang Huang hsien-sheng wen-chi* (abbreviated *YCHHSWC*), 19–204a. Note the metaphor borrowed from Taoist alchemy.

20. 26–251b; 28–13a; 165.

21. 31–291a; 33–1b; 187.

22. 8–81b; 9–7a.

23. 35–328b; 36–5a.

24. *WMK*, 292–c.

25. Ibid., 292–b;

26. 38–363a; 39–6a.

27. *CCC*, 80–673a.

28. Ibid., 81–675a.

29. *SPTK*, Ssu-K'ung T'u, *Ssu-K'ung piao-sheng wen-chi*, 2, 9–a.

30. *CCC*, 77–652a. Yang quotes from the *Shih-ching, Kuo-feng*, no. 35, "Ku Feng," lines 13 and 14.

31. Ibid., 79–666b.

32. Ibid., 83–690ab. The lines Yang quotes are from *Shih-ching, Hsiao-ya*, no. 199, "Ho Jen Ssu," and, of course, Yang follows tradition in interpreting the poem as a political allegory.

33. *CTCTL*, 335–c.

34. *Taisho, Yüan-wu Fo-kuo ch'an-shih yü-lu*, no. 1997, vol. 47, p. 782–a. It is interesting to note that Yang's mentor Chang Chün, wrote one of the prefaces to this work.

35. *CCC*, 80–672b.

36. *CTCTL*, 290–b.

37. *CCC*, 80–673b.

38. Ibid., 80–673b.

39. Ibid., 81–675b.

40. Yeh Hsieh, *Yüan Shih*, in *Ch'ing shih-hua*, ed. Ting Fu-pao (Peking: Chung-hua shu-chü, 1963), vol. 2, p. 606.

41. Lü Liu-liang et al., ed., *Sung shih ch'ao* (Shanghai: Commercial Press, 1935), vol. 3, p. 1871.

42. *WMK*, 295–a.

43. *CTCTL*, 263–b.

44. 26–248b; 28–10b; 161. The word "them" in the first line refers to the boatmen mentioned in the previous poem.

45. Literally, "the place joined, paper scar streak." (25–242a; 28–4a; 158.)

46. 40–382a; 41–2a; 232.

47. 40–382a; 41–2a; 233.

48. Ibid. The Fat Immortal was a *hao* or literary name used by Chang Lei, who was noted for his rotundity.

49. Kuo Shao-yü, ed., and with a commentary by, *Ts'ang-lang shih-hua chiao-shih* (abbreviated *TLSHCS*) (Peking: Jen-min wen-hsüeh ch'u-pan she, 1962), p. 54. The entire work has been translated into German with exhaustive commentary and an excellent introduction in Günther Debon, *Ts'ang Lang's Gespräche über die Dichtung* (Wiesbaden, 1962).

50. Ibid., p. 10. See Debon, p. 57.

51. Ibid., p. 24. See Debon, p. 62, where he translates *shen-k'o* "einschneidend."

52. Ibid., p. 1.

53. Ibid., p. 10. See Debon, p. 57. The word *wu* is translated as a noun, which does not seem to correspond with the Chinese.

54. 26–251b; 28–13a; 165.

55. Ibid., p. 1. I have not been able to determine what the four Music Bureau, or *Yüeh-fu*, poems are. See Debon, p. 59.

56. Yeh Hsieh, *Yüan-shih*, 3, 599.

Chapter Three

1. Chang Tzu, *Nan-hu chi*, chuan 7, 22–a, in *Chih-pu tsu-chai ts'ung-shu* (1921).

2. Chou Pi-ta, *Chou Yi-kuo Wen-chung-kung chi* (1848), "P'ing-yüan hsü-kao," *chüan* 1, "Tz'u-yün Yang T'ing-hsiu tai-chih chi-t'i chu-shih Huan-jan Shu-yüan."

3. *YWLHC*, pp. 5–19. Although I have found Chou Ju-ch'ang's discussion of the live method useful, my treatment is totally different.

4. Liu K'o-chuang, *Hou-ts'un hsien-sheng ta ch'üan-chi*, 95–826a.

5. Ibid., 95–822b.

6. Ko T'ien-min, *Ko Wu-huai hsiao-chi*, in *Chi-ku-ko ying-ch'ao Nan-Sung liu-shih chia chi*, "Chi Yang Ch'eng-chai." The sword Ko mentions is so sharp it will cut hairs when they are blown against it. Ko means that Yang's poetry achieves its effects without any visible effort.

7. Nāgārjuna, *Madhyamakaśāstra* (Darbhanga: Mithila Institute, 1961), p. 4.

8. 12–112b; 13–4b; 100.

9. *CCC*, 114–988ab. Meng Chia was a scholar from the Tsin dynasty noted for his wild behavior. One day while he was attending a banquet, the wind blew his hat off, but in accordance with his romantic nature, he did not pay attention to this. See *Tsin-shu*, *chüan* 98, p. 1341b. For "public cases" see the following discussion.

10. The mid-autumn festival was held on the fifteenth of the eighth lunar month.

11. 7–67a; 8–1a; 64.

12. *CCC*, 114–989ab.

13. Li Po, *Fen-lei pu-chu Li T'ai-po shih* (abbreviated *LTPS*), SPTK, 23–313a.

14. 36–345b; 37–8b.

15. 25–233a; 27–6b.

16. Yen K'o-chün, ed., *Ch'üan Shang-ku San-tai Ch'in Han San-kuo Liu-ch'ao wen* (Taipei: Shih-chieh shu-chü reprint, 1968), vol. 6, *Ch'üan Ch'i wen*, *chüan* 19, p. 8.

17. 14–127b; 15–1a.

18. *LTPS*, 7–134b.

19. 19–183b; 21–10b.

20. *WMK*, 297b.

21. Raven silver is an allusion to a poem of Meng Chiao, in which he compares charcoal to raven silver. See *Meng Tung-yeh chi*, SPPY, 9–4b.

22. 28–261a; 30–1a; 177.

23. 21–201a; 23–6a.

24. *Taisho*, *Miao-fa lien-hua ching*, no. 262, vol. 9, p. 20–c.

25. 26–247b; 28–9b; 161.

26. Sincere Study was the name of Yang's library.

27. 37–356b; 38–9b; 224.

28. 25–239b; 28–1b.

29. 15–138b; 16–2b; 116.

30. 11–108b; 12–9a.

31. 18–166a; 20–2b.

32. The *t'u-mi* is a member of the rose family.

33. 25–236a; 27–9b.

34. 32–306a; 34–7a.

35. *WMK*, 293b.

36. Wei Ch'ing-chih, *Shih-jen yü-hsieh*, p. 121.

37. Quoted on p. 6 of *YWLHC*. The original source has not been available to me.

38. *CCC*, 114–987a.

39. 26–248b; 28–10b.

40. *CCC*, 114–987a.

41. 11–108a; 12–8a.

42. 18–169b; 20–6a; 127.

43. 13–123b; 14–5a; 105.

44. Liu K'o-chuang, *Hou-ts'un hsien-sheng ta ch'üan chi*, SPTK, 97–844ab.

45. *Taisho, Chen-chou Lin-chi Hui-chao ch'an-shih yü-lu*, no. 1985, vol. 47, p. 503-b. The entire work has been translated into French in Paul Demiéville, *Entretiens de Lin-tsi* (Paris: Librairie Artheme Fayard, 1972), p. 180.

46. The last line of the poem translated literally reads: "If he is angry, how can I avoid it?" Note the highly colloquial use of *tu* for "how" (5–45b; 5–2a; 50).

47. 10–100a; 11–10b; 92.

48. Lü Liu-liang, et al., ed., *Sung-shih ch'ao* (Shanghai: Commercial Press, 1935), vol. 3, p. 1871.

49. 42–408b; 42–14b.

50. Lo Ta-ching, *Ho-lin yü-lu*, in *Pi-chi hsiao-shuo ta-kuan hsü-pien* (Taipei: Hsin-hsing shu-chü, 1962), *chüan* 3, p. 4a, p. 2290.

51. Chu Yi-tsun, *P'u-shu t'ing chi*, SPTK, 38–319a.

52. Ibid., 52–412b.

Chapter Four

1. 39–377b; 40–11a; 229.

2. *Taisho, Ta-chih tu-lun*, no. 1509, vol. 25, p. 101-c.

3. Ibid., 102–b. This passage has been translated and annotated in E. Lamotte's monumental *Le Traité de la grande vertu de sagesse de Nāgārjuna* (Louvain, 1944), vol. 1, p. 364.

4. Ting Fu-pao, ed., *Ch'üan Han San-kuo Chin Nan-pei Ch'ao shih* (Taipei: Shih-chieh shu-chü, 1962), vol. 2, p. 907. According to Chinese mythology the moon contains a hare and a cassia tree.

5. In this poem we find two allusions to the four poems of Li Po entitled "Drinking Alone Beneath the Moon." See *LTPS*, 23–313ab. "The sky loves wine" is from the first two lines of the poem: "If the sky did not love wine/ The Wine Star would not be in the sky." "The moon doesn't know how to drink" is a direct quotation from the fifth line of the first poem. The second

line from the last is somewhat puzzling, and an alternative translation would be: "How do I know that through the myriad ages there is only a single material body?" (36–345b; 37–8b; 218).

6. Lo Ta-ching, *Ho-lin yü-lu*, in *Pi-chi hsiao-shuo ta-kuan hsü-pien* (Taipei: Hsin-hsing shu-chü, 1962), *chüan* 10, p. 10–b, p. 2313.

7. 40–379a; 40–12b; 230.

8. Mister No-such is one of the three fantastic characters in the Han poet Ssu-ma Hsiang-ju's *Tzu-hsü fu*. See the poet's biography and *fu* in *Shih-chi, chüan* 117 (12–110a; 13–1b; 98).

9. 27–256a; 29–4b.

10. 29–277a; 31–8a.

11. 32–303b; 34–4a; 192.

Chapter Five

1. *SPTK*, T'ao Ch'ien, *Chien-chu T'ao Yüan-ming chi* (abbreviated *CCTYMC*), 3–37a. Translated in J. R. Hightower, *The Poetry of T'ao Ch'ien* (Oxford: Clarendon Press, 1970), pp. 163–65.

2. *SPTK*, Tu Fu, *Tu Kung-pu shih* (abbreviated *TKPS*) 1–53a.

3. Allusion to Tu Fu's poem: "From afar I pity my little sons and daughters/ For they do not yet know enough to think of me at Ch'ang-an." See *A Concordance to the Poems of Tu Fu* (abbreviated *TF*), *Harvard-Yenching Sinological Index Series*, Supplement No. 14, (reprint, Taipei, 1966), 295/6/4.

4. 1–8b; 1–6a; 13.

5. 16–145b; 17–1b.

6. Allusion to the *Lan-t'ing chi-hsü* of the great calligrapher Wang Hsi-chih (321–379) in which Wang and his friends floated wine cups in a small stream on the *shang-ssu* festival.

7. 40–385b; 41–12b.

8. Mei Yao-ch'en, *Wan-ling hsien-sheng chi*, *SPTK*, 28–243b. Mei's poem "Drinking with my Wife at Night on the Boat" is the earliest Chinese poem I know of that suggests that accompanying one's wife could be more stimulating than male companionship!

9. Li Shang-yin, *Li Yi-shan shih chi*, *SPTK*, 1–1b.

10. The leek is used to describe delicate fingers. The parrot is most likely some decoration and not a real bird.

11. 25–238b; 27–12b; 156.

12. *CCTYMC*, 2–15b–17a. Translated in Hightower, p. 50–56.

13. *Lao-tzu tao-te ching*, *SPTK*, 1–8b.

14. *Jui-hsiang*, or lucky incense, is *Daphne odora*; *hsüan-ts'ao Hemerocallis flava* or "daylily," *han, Nasturtium*. All of these plants were popular with Sung gardeners.

15. Golden Valley Villa was the famous garden of the Tsin dynasty mul-

timillionaire, Shih Ch'ung (249–300), who was notorious for his extravagance and cruelty.

16. 20–189a; 22–4b; 141.

17. See Li Chih, *Fen Shu* (Peking: Chung-hua shu-chü, 1961), pp. 97–99.

18. 24–229a; 27–2b; 153.

19. Before glass was widespread in China, most windows were pasted over with paper as in many Japanese houses today.

20. 17–156a; 19–2a; 125.

21. According to his biography, at one time the poet Ssu-ma Hsiang-ju (179–117 B.C.) was so poor that "Living at home, only the four walls stood around him." See *Shih-chi*, K'ai-ming shu-chü, 254–c.

22. Allusion to the *CTCTL*: "A monk asked Medicine Mountain 'Why do you read sutras?' The master replied, 'I just use them to screen my eyes!' " See *CTCTL*, p. 312–b. Yang means he just puts books in front of his face without actually reading them.

23. Fly heads are finely written characters, whereas "old ravens" are sloppy writing.

24. "Fishnet paper" is paper of high quality such as the inventor of paper in Han times, Ts'ai Lun, is supposed to have made from cloth and fish nets. Tadpole-head writing actually refers to characters in the archaic seal script, but here Yang only means fine writing.

25. Sung editions were printed from hand-carved wooden blocks, which frequently imitated the writing style of famous calligraphers. "Sparse and lean" is a reference to the style of calligraphy popular in early T'ang times and highly prized by Sung collectors.

26. Yang may mean more than just ordinary plants here, for flowers and willows were symbols for prostitutes.

27. An allusion to Huang-fu Shih's (fl. 813) preface to Ku K'uang's (d. ca. 814) complete works: "His free songs and long lines loftily burst forth and explode, frequently piercing to heaven's heart, going beyond the moon's ribs, and startling people beyond their expectations; his language is not ordinary!" See Huang-fu Shih, *Huang-fu Ch'ih-cheng chi*, 2–7b.

28. A reference to a poem by Tu Fu: "In a moment a nine-layer true dragon [horse] comes out/ And washes all the ordinary horses of the age empty [deflates them]." See *TF*, 121/12/24.

29. The Taoist elixir of immortality, which could cure all diseases and eliminate old age.

30. 16–147a; 17–3a; 119.

31. Literally, "Uncle Joy," another name for wine.

32. Reference to the four dormant periods of silk worms before they spin their cocoons.

33. 1–10b; 1–8a; 14.

34. 12–114a; 13–6a.

35. The counters were used in playing drinking games.

36. Allusion to a story from *Lieh-tzu*: "There was a man by the sea who loved seagulls, and every morning he would go to the seaside and follow the seagulls around. All the seagulls came, perching there without fear. His father said to him, 'I hear that the seagulls all follow you around. Bring me one so I can play with it.' The next day he went to the seaside, but the seagulls soared around him and would not come down." See *Ch'ung-hsü chih-te chen-ching, SPTK*, 2–8a. Yang is saying that although he does not have any false schemes like the man in the story, there still are people like the peasant who are suspicious of him and keep their distance.

37. 5–46a; 5–2b; 51.

38. 18–166a; 20–2b; 126.

39. Both plants are round like coins with colors like gold and copper, respectively.

40. 14–132b; 15–6a; 113.

41. Hsieh T'iao (464–499) was a famous poet of the Southern Ch'i dynasty, who once built a house on the mountain. Li Po, who greatly admired Hsieh, was buried to the northwest of the mountain.

42. Summoning back Li Po's soul is a reference to shamanistic practices popular in Chinese folk religion until modern times.

43. The Immortal of Poetry is a title commonly given to Li Po. I have accepted Chou Ju-ch'ang's emendation of the text of this poem (32–312a; 35–1a; 197).

44. A large seal was the sign of high official position.

45. From Chuang-tzu: "Confucians use a metal club to bash his chin." See *Nan-hua chen-ching, SPTK*, 9–193b. Yang is saying people frequently endanger their lives in the search for high office.

46. Juan Chi (210–263) of the Tsin dynasty and Li Po of the T'ang were both famous for their drinking and reckless behavior.

47. 10–95a; 11–5a; 86.

48. The green flag was commonly hung outside inns and bars from at least T'ang times onwards.

49. 26–249a; 28–10b; 162.

50. Yoshikawa Kōjirō, *Sōshi Gaisetsu*, in *Chūgoku Shijin Senshū* (Tokyo: Iwanami Shoten, 1962), pp. 27–29. Translated by Burton Watson in *An Introduction to Sung Poetry*, (Cambridge: Harvard University Press, 1967), pp. 19–21.

51. See Burton Watson, *Early Chinese Literature* (New York: Columbia University Press, 1962), pp. 202–3.

52. Ibid., pp. 289–90.

53. See the poet's preface to his *Hsin Yüeh-fu*, in SPTK, Po Chü-yi, *Po-shih ch'ang-ch'ing chi* (abbreviated *PSCCC*), 31–17a.

54. A bamboo branch song is a form of folk song which originated in

Szechwan and later became popular among upper class poets in T'ang times after Liu Yü-hsi composed imitations.

55. 26–249b; 28–11b; 164.

56. Po Chü-yi's collection is filled with this type of poem, but the most famous are in the *Hsin Yüeh-fu* form. For the sake of comparison, one could read Po's "Old Man of Tu-ling" in which the poet criticizes excessive taxation. Although Po obviously pities the poor peasants, he utilizes the overworked stereotype of the rapacious tax collector, and his interest in the peasant is predominantly political. See *PSCCC*, 4–22c.

57. The boat people, or Tanka, are found along the sea in South China and are quite numerous in modern Hong Kong. They were formerly despised as a minority race and were prohibited from living on dry land.

58. The father is in a hurry, because he knows that his family is prohibited from setting foot on dry land, and the reeds required for fuel are only temporarily flooded.

59. 16–149b; 18–1a; 123.

60. As one would expect, Li Po was particularly fascinated by boat women, an interest possibly aroused by their dealings in prostitution. See particularly the second, third, and fourth poems of Li's "Songs on the Women of Yüeh" in *LTPS*, 25–348b.

61. *CCTYMC*, 10–92b.

62. In other words, there has just been a heavy rainfall.

63. In this line Yang is comparing himself to a friend of Tu Fu, Cheng Ch'ien (d. ca. 761), who held the post of Doctor of the Kuang-wen College. Tu presented Cheng a poem in which he described Cheng's poverty: "Master Kuang-wen's rice is not sufficient." See *TF*, 14/18/4.

64. The wheat crop is almost a total loss, and the rice is still too young to eat.

65. 2–19b; 2–6b; 33.

66. See Po's poem "Watching the Planting" in *PSCCC*, 6–32c.

67. Chang Tsai, *Chang-tzu ch'üan-shu SPPY*, 1–1a and 1–3a.

68. 6–62b; 7–5a; 61.

69. Literally, "they don't like affairs." The words *hao-shih* were used to describe individuals interested in curious affairs and even the arts.

70. 32–306b; 34–7b; 195.

71. Beating the spring ox was a widespread custom in Sung times. On the first day of spring a mud ox was made, ceremonially beaten, and then broken into pieces to insure a rich harvest. The mud of the ox was even felt to be efficacious in treating various diseases.

72. In the ceremony Yang witnessed, there obviously was a statue of a boy, too.

73. Fields of ripe wheat resemble clouds in the sky, and the wheat tassels look like broom heads.

74. 12–113b; 13–5a; 101.

75. When planting rice seedlings, the seedlings are first tied into small bundles.

76. 13–124b; 14–6a; 107.

77. 34–323a; 35–12a; 207.

78. For examples from the Southern Sung contemporary with Yang Wan-li, see *SJHT*, plate no. 29, and *Slides of Chinese Painting in the National Palace Museum* (abbreviated *NPM*), E List, slide no. 2.

79. *Dai Nippon Zoku Zōkyō*, Shih-niu t'u-sung, second *pien*, first *chi*, *t'ao* 18, vol. 5, p. 461.

80. Ibid.

81. There is a study of the relation between the ox or water buffalo and Ch'an Buddhism in Dotane Ken'yu, "Ushi to Zensō," *Zen Bunka*, no. 67 (December, 1972), pp. 14–20. After studying the background of the ox in Chinese religion and philosophy he proceeds to discuss ox-herding poems by Sung Ch'an masters and the relation of these poems to Sung paintings. Yang's good friend Lu Yu also made use of the herding theme, for in a poem to Hsin Ch'i-chi he wrote: "You have meditated on and penetrated the Southern Patriarch's talk about herding oxen." See *LFWCC*, 57–4b.

Chapter Six

1. Lake Po-yang is one of the great lakes of China, situated in northern Kiangsi province.

2. Another name for lake Po-yang.

3. Mount Lu was a center of Buddhist monasteries and within view of T'ao Ch'ien's native village.

4. See discussion on p. 61. Yang wants to leave society for his own sake. (14–127b; 15–1a; 110.)

5. James Cahill, *Chinese Painting* (Switzerland: Skira, 1960), p. 25.

6. Reproduced in color in Francois Fourcade, *Art Treasures of the Peking Museum* (New York: Abrams, 1965), p. 29, plate 1.

7. *Lao-tzu tao-te ching*, SPTK, 1–5a.

8. Many of Han Yü's poems display the malevolence of nature, his "Meng Chiao's Son Died" being an excellent example. See Han Yü, *Chu Wen-Kung chiao Ch'ang-li hsien-sheng chi*, SPTK, 4–43b.

9. The most famous example is Lu T'ung's "Poem on a Lunar Eclipse." See *Yü ch'uan-tzu shih chi*, SPTK, 1–2a–3b. This has been translated in A. C. Graham, *Poems of the Late T'ang* (Harmondsworth, England: Penguin Books, 1966).

10. Li Ho, *Li Ho Ko-shih pien*, SPTK, 4–25b; translated by Graham, ibid., p. 117.

11. 10–97a; 11–7a; 90.

12. Instead of "boatmen" the original Chinese has *huang-mao-lang*, or "yellow hat lads," which according to Chou Ju-ch'ang is another term for "boatmen." Since the poet states they are wearing purple bamboo caps in the next line, I have not translated literally.

13. Allusion to the raven which was supposed to inhabit the sun.

14. 27–260a; 29–8b; 176.

15. 11–104a; 12–4b; 94.

16. For Fan K'uan, see Cahill, *Chinese Painting,* pp. 32–34. Also Osvald Siren, *Chinese Painting, Leading Masters and Principles* (London: Lund Humphries, 1956–1958), vol. 1, pp. 201–7.

17. For Kuo Hsi, see Cahill, pp. 35–38; see also Siren, vol. 1, pp. 196–201.

18. One of the most magnificent surviving examples of this kind of Northern Sung landscape painting is Fan K'uan's, *Traveling Among Streams and Mountains,* reproduced in Cahill, ibid., p. 33.

19. See *Early Spring,* reproduced in ibid., p. 36.

20. *TPHSS,* 12–230b.

21. For Ma Yüan, see Cahill, pp. 80–82, and Siren, vol. 2, pp. 113–19.

22. See Cahill, pp. 82–84, and Siren, vol. 2, pp. 119–24.

23. See Cahill, p. 38.

24. Ibid., p. 84. Cahill does not openly state the relationship between the Ma-Hsia school and Ch'an painters, but his reference to "impressions of spontaneous disclosure" in Hsia Kuei's paintings sounds remarkably Ch'anist.

25. Typical examples of this kind of painting by Ma Yüan are reproduced in Cahill, pp. 82, 83. See also *NPM,* P List, no. 3, *Facing the Moon* by Ma Yüan.

26. 35–336a; 36–12b.

27. 33–313a; 35–2a; 201.

28. *LTPS,* 23–318a.

29. Sunspots were thought to be a raven inhabiting the sun.

30. The White Moon-beauty, or Su-e, is another name for Ch'ang-e, the immortal woman who lives on the moon.

31. The morning star, Venus.

32. The moon was said to have a cassia tree and a hare that pounded the medicine of immortality.

33. The red brocade is the glow of the dawn sky.

34. The poet is comparing the red disk of the early sun to red-colored hub caps on a chariot wheel.

35. 25–241b; 28–3b; 158.

36. The East Ministry is the Mi-shu Sheng, or Imperial Library, where Yang was serving at the time.

37. Allusion to the Tsin poet Juan Chi (210–263), who would make his eyes black if he liked someone and white if he disliked the person. In this line and those following, Yang is describing the changes in the moon as it grows dimmer in the morning light and is covered with clouds.

38. The morning star, Venus.

39. A raven is supposed to live on the sun. Yang compares sunlight to red dragon scales (23–218b; 25–6a; 146).

40. *LTPS*, 23–313a.

41. 35–330b; 36–6b; 212.

42. 32–307a; 34–8a; 196.

43. An excellent example of this kind of painting, in addition to those cited above, is a landscape by Hsia Kuei, reproduced in *SJHT*, plate no. 50. Although the men in the painting are completely at ease in a friendly landscape, almost half of the scene is obscured in clouds.

44. 32–304b; 34–5a; 193.

45. 40–384a; 41–4a.

46. Yang is describing a bridge made from wooden beams joined together so that the ends stick out from the sides of the bridge like the legs of a centipede.

47. Literally, "An ox recognizes me as his herding boy."

48. 34–319b; 35–8b; 205.

49. 32–304a; 34–5a; 193.

50. Reproduced in Cahill, p. 82.

51. *Lao-tzu tao-te ching*, *SPTK*, 1–4a.

52. *Taisho, Miao-fa lien-hua ching* (abbreviated *MFLHC*), no. 262, vol. 9, p. 5–b.

53. *CCTYMC*, 3–30a.

54. 42–401a; 42–7a.

55. 26–249a; 28–11a.

56. The Shu area of modern Szechwan and Wu of Kiangsu were both famous for their textiles. Yang is comparing the evening colors to these fine cloths.

57. A direct quotation of the Southern Ch'i poet Hsieh T'iao's most famous line. See Ting Fu-pao, *Ch'üan Han San-kuo Chin Nan-pei-ch'ao shih* (Taipei: Shih-chieh shu-chü, 1961), p. 811 (26–250b; 28–12b; 164).

58. *Shen-t'ung* translates Sanskrit *rddhi-pāda* or "spiritual power."

59. *Tūla* is Sanskrit for "cotton."

60. The sun is obscured by the mist so it seems to be a red platter hanging in the sky.

61. A *stūpa* is a hemispherical structure of brick or wood used to contain relics of the Buddha or his disciples.

62. Mount E-mei in Szechwan was a common goal for pilgrims with its many famous Buddhist temples.

63. 34–320b; 35–9b.

64. *MFLHC*, p. 32–b.

65. Ibid., p. 32–c.

66. *CTCTL*, p. 270–b.

67. *Dai Nippon Zoku Zōkyō, Ku tsun su yü-lu*, second *pien*, first *chi*, *t'ao* 31, vol. 3, *chüan* 32, p. 228.

68. *Taisho, Hsiao-p'in mo-ho pan-jo po-lo-mi ching*, no. 227, vol. 8, p. 540c.

69. A color reproduction of a particularly striking example found re-

cently in China appears in *Wen-hua ta ko-ming ch'i-chien ch'u-t'u wen-wu* (Peking: Wen-wu ch'u-pan-she, 1972).

70. See the chapter "Ju shan fu" in *SPTK, Pao-p'u-tzu*, 17–99b–106b. This chapter is translated in J. R. Ware, *Alchemy, Medicine and Religion, in the China of A.D. 320*, (Cambridge: M.I.T. Press, 1966).

71. "Following the Chin-chu Torrent, I Cross the Mountain Range, and Walk Beside a Stream," in Hsieh Ling-yün, *Hsieh K'ang-le shih chu* (Taipei: Yi-wen Yin-shu-kuan).

72. *Lun-yü, SPTK*, 4–29a.

73. Wang Wei, *Wang Yu-ch'eng chi, SPTK*, 4–37b.

74. Refer to the paintings already cited. Ma Yüan was particularly noted for his balancing of solid landscape against empty mist and received the nickname "Side-corner Ma" from this type of composition.

75. See the Eastern Han bronze horse reproduced in *Wen-wu*, no. 2, 1972.

76. See, for example, the recently discovered lacquer paintings of paragons of filial piety from the Northern Wei reproduced in *Wen-wu*, no. 3 (1972), plate no. 11. Ku K'ai-chih's renowned *Admonitions to the Court Ladies*, presently in the British Museum and supposedly painted in the fourth century, is also didactic.

77. *SPTK, Nan-hua chen-ching*, 6–128a; translated in Burton Watson, *The Complete Works of Chuang Tzu* (Columbia University Press, 1968), pp. 188–89.

78. See Kenneth Ch'en, *Buddhism in China* (Princeton: Princeton University Press, 1964), p. 39.

79. *Shih-ching, Kuo-feng*, "Kuan-chü."

80. *TKPS*, 23–402b.

81. It is interesting to note that Tu Fu's most famous poem about painting, "The Ballad of Painting" or "Tan Ch'ing Yin," is concerned with an eighth-century horse painter Ts'ao Pa, who was the teacher of Han Kan. See *TKPS*, 16–287a.

82. The zoology of the poem is quite confusing. It is not clear whether the water mantis is a separate species or merely a praying mantis that has somehow landed in the water.

83. 35–334b; 36–11a; 213.

84. 34–324b; 36–1b; 207.

85. 10–94a; 11–4a; 85.

86. 34–325a; 36–2a; 208.

87. 13–126b; 14–8a; 109.

88. 11–103b; 12–3b; 93.

89. See the discussion of the scientific elements in Chu Hsi's thought in Joseph Needham, *Science and Civilization in China* (Cambridge: Cambridge University Press, 1961), vol. 2, pp. 493–96. Chu's extremely scientific cosmology is outlined on pp. 373–74.

90. Quoted from Feng Yu-lan, *A History of Chinese Philosophy* (Prince-

ton: Princeton University Press, 1953), vol. 2, p. 406. This passage does not appear in the Chinese original and must have been one of the revisions Feng made for the translation.

91. Some liberty has been taken with the word *sheng*, which Chou Ju-ch'ang interprets as a verb. 11–103a; 12–3a; 93.

92. 36–345a; 37–8a; 218.

93. Here I have followed the *SPPY* reading.

94. The Queen Mother or Hsi Wang Mu was a mythical woman who lived in a paradise to the west of China.

95. Raven Robe Valley is a place in modern Kiangsu province, where the ancient aristocrats of the Wang and Hsieh families lived in Tsin times. By Yang's age all of the former glory had disappeared.

96. 12–112a; 13–3b.

97. Reproduced in Cahill, p. 72.

98. "This gentleman" is an allusion to Wang Hui-chih's biography in the *Tsin-shu:* "Once when he was living in an empty house, he had bamboos planted. Someone asked him the reason for this, but he only chanted back, 'How could I be without this gentleman even one day?' " See *Tsin-shu*, K'ai-ming shu-chü, 12, 91–d.

99. Wen T'ung, who lived in northern Sung times, was famous for his bamboo paintings.

100. 26–243a; 28–4b; 159.

101. 34–318b; 35–7b.

102. 37–355b; 38–8b.

103. *YCHHSWC*, 3–30b.

104. 9–89b; 10–7b; 83.

105. The "whiskers" of the plum are the stamens of its flower.

106. 12–114b; 13–6b; 102.

107. 39–375b; 40–8b.

108. Translated for the greater part in Li Ju-chen, *Flowers in the Mirror*, trans. Lin Tai-yi (Berkeley: University of California Press, 1965).

Chapter Seven

1. Yoshikawa Kōjirō, *Sōshi Gaisetsu*, pp. 34–39; translated in Burton Watson, *An Introduction to Sung Poetry*, pp. 24–28.

2. Literally, "Now that I know commands," which is an allusion to Confucius' *Analects:* "At fifty I knew heaven's commands." See *Lun Yü*, *SPTK*, 1–5b.

3. 10–96b; 11–6b; 89.

4. Su Shih, *Ching-chin Tung-p'o wen-chi shih-lüeh*, *SPTK*, 1–13a.

5. 9–87b; 10–5a; 80.

6. The first line of the second of two poems by Su Shih entitled "Reading Meng Chiao's Poetry" states: "I despise Meng Chiao's poetry!" *TPHSS*, 25–465b.

7. T'ang Kuei-chang, ed., *Ch'üan Sung Tz'u* (Peking: Chung-hua shu-chü, 1965), p. 288.

8. I have followed the *SPPY* reading in the title.

9. A reference to the author's recent appointment to a post in Kuang-tung.

10. Literally, "the first watch," which lasted roughly from eight to nine o'clock. (15–137a; 16–1b; 115.)

11. The boat's kitchen is at the rear of the boat, so the favorable wind blows the smoke toward the front.

12. 35–326b; 36–3a; 210.

13. For the growth of the Chinese economy in Sung times see Mark Elvin, *The Pattern of the Chinese Past* (Stanford: Stanford University Press, 1973).

14. Lung-yu was in the general area of modern Kansu province. The district had been devastated by recent rebellions.

15. Pa and Shu are modern Szechwan. Tu is referring to recent invasions by Tibetan and other non-Chinese tribes.

16. *TKPS*, 261b.

17. 34–325b; 36–2a; 209.

18. The last two lines of the last poem of five entitled "Written While Drunk on the Twenty-seventh of the Sixth Month at the Tower for Watching the Lake." *TPHSS*, 9–184b.

19. Meng Chiao, *Meng Tung-ye chi, SPPY*, 4–1a.

20. 25–233a; 27–6b; 153.

21. 34–325b; 36–2a; 209.

22. 24–228a; 27–1b; 153.

23. Reference to a famous line by Li Po: "The moon does not know how to drink." See p. 61.

24. 25–233a; 27–6b; 153.

Chapter Eight

1. For an excellent treatment of Li Chih and late Ming thought in general, see William Theodore de Bary, "Individualism and Humanitarianism" in *Self and Society in Ming Thought* (New York: Columbia University Press, 1970), pp. 188–222 in particular.

2. Yuan Hung-tao, *Yüan Chung-lang ch'üan chi* (Shanghai: Shih-chieh shu-chü, 1935), *chüan* 1, pp. 5–6.

3. Yüan Mei, *Sui-yüan shih-hua* (Peking: Jen-min wen-hsüeh ch'u-pan she, 1960), *chüan* 1, p. 2.

4. Ibid., *chüan* 8, p. 272.

Selected Bibliography

PRIMARY SOURCES

1. Only the two following editions of Yang Wan-li's works are easily available.

   Ch'eng-chai chi, Ssu-pu ts'ung-k'an, (Taipei: Commercial Press reprint,) which contains both Yang's poetry and prose works.

   Ch'eng-chai shih chi, Ssu-pu pei-yao, (Taipei: Chung-hua shu-chü reprint, 1970,) which contains only Yang's poetry.

2. The most valuable annotated selection of Yang Wan-li's poetry already mentioned.

   Chou Ju-ch'ang, *Yang Wan-li hsüan-chi,* (Peking: Chung-hua shu-chü, 1964.)

3. A very useful collection of source materials relating to Yang Wan-li and his friend Fan Ch'eng-ta.

   Yang Wan-li Fan Ch'eng-ta chüan, (Peking: Chung-hua shu-chü, 1965.)

Specialists should refer to the footnotes above for the many other works in Chinese which are of use in the study of Yang Wan-li's poetry. The following is a small list of books published in European languages that would be helpful for the general reader in gaining a more complete understanding of Yang's times and Sung poetry.

SECONDARY SOURCES

CH'EN, KENNETH. *Buddhism in China.* Princeton: Princeton University Press, 1964.

DEBON, GÜNTHER. *Ts'ang Langs Gespräche über die Dichtung.* Wiesbaden: Otto Harrassowitz, 1962.

DEMIEVILLE, PAUL. *Entretiens de Lin-tsi.* Paris: Librairie Arthème Fayard, 1972.

FAN CH'ENG-TA. *The Golden Year of Fan Ch'eng-ta.* Translated by Gerald Bullet. Cambridge: Cambridge University Press, 1946.

FUNG YU-LAN. *A History of Chinese Philosophy.* Princeton: Princeton University Press, 1953.

GERNET, JACQUES. *Daily Life in China on the Eve of the Mongol Invasion.*
    New York: MacMillan, 1962.
LIU, JAMES J. Y. *Major Lyricists of the Northern Sung.* Princeton: Princeton
    University Press, 1974.
———. *Chinese Theories of Literature.* Chicago: University of Chicago
    Press, 1975.
LIU, WU-CHI, and LO, IRVING YU-CHENG, eds. *Sunflower Splendor: Three
    Thousand Years of Chinese Poetry.* New York: Anchor Press, 1975.
LO, IRVING YU-CHENG. *Hsin Ch'i-chi.* New York: Twayne Publishers, 1971.
SU SHIH. *Su Tung-p'o, Selections from a Sung Dynasty Poet.* Translated by
    Burton Watson. New York: Columbia University Press, 1966.
WATSON, BURTON. *Chinese Lyricism.* New York: Columbia University
    Press, 1971.
YOSHIKAWA KOJIRO. *An Introduction to Sung Poetry.* Translated by Burton
    Watson. Cambridge, Mass.: Harvard University Press, 1967.

Index

Analects, The, 123
Asta-sāhāsrikā-prajñā-pāramitā Sūtra, 123

Ch'an Buddhism, 21, 25, 26, 30, 34, 37–40, 43, 48, 50, 54, 55, 57, 58, 67, 71, 87, 90, 101, 117, 120–22, 124, 129, 130, 145, 147
Chang Chün, 17, 18, 20, 21, 30, 32
Chang Lei, 52
Chang Shih, 24
Chang Tsai, 99, 129
Chang Tzu, 56
Chao-chou, 50
Ch'en Shih-tao, 40, 41, 44, 47, 53
Ch'en Yen, 69
Ch'eng-chai chi, 36
Chien-wen Ti, 79
Ch'in Kuei, 17, 18
Ching Hua Yüan, 135
Ching-te ch'uan-teng lu, 38, 90
Chou Ju-ch'ang, 56
Chou Pi-ta, 50, 56, 57
Chü-chih, 68, 71
Chu Hsi, 92, 129
Ch'u Kuang-hsi, 40
Chu Yi-tsun, 76, 77
Chuang-tzu, 125
Classic of Poetry (Shih-ching), 95, 103, 125, 144

fa, 57–58
fan-an, 61–62
Fan Ch'eng-ta, 15, 16, 46
Fan K'uan, 108
Fuo-kuo, 48

Han Chü, 39–40
Han Kan, 126
Han Shih-chung, 32
Han T'o-chou, 35–36
Han Yü, 44, 53, 69, 106, 136
Hsia Kuei, 109
Hsiao Te-tsao, 19, 76
Hsiao-tsung, 19–21, 24, 29–32, 35
Hsieh K'o, 47
Hsieh Ling-yün, 44, 103, 123
Hsü Ssu-sun, 72
Hsü Ssu-tao, 72
Hsieh T'iao, 119
Hsieh Yi, 47
Hsin Ch'i-chi, 16
Hsü Fu, 47
Huang Ch'üan, 125
Huang-po, 49, 122
Huang T'ing-chien, 19, 44, 47, 52, 53, 71, 72, 76, 133, 136
Hui-k'ai, 43, 74
Hui-neng, 43
Hui Shih, 125
huo-fa, 56
Hung Ch'u, 47
Hung P'eng, 47
Hung Yen, 47
Hung-jen, 43

Kao Ho, 47
Kao-tsung, 15, 17, 19
Kiangsi School, 19, 40, 41, 44, 47, 52, 53, 56, 72, 136
Ko T'ien-min, 58, 65
ko-wu, 106, 129
Kuang-tsung, 29, 31, 32, 35

Kumārajīva, 79
kung-an, 62
K'ung Chih-kuei, 61
Kuo Hsi, 108, 110, 111, 115

Lao-tzu, 106
Li Ch'eng, 110
Li Chih, 88, 147
Li Ho, 106–108, 137
Li Ling, 50, 54
Li Po, 53, 54, 61, 62, 74, 76, 94, 111,
    113, 114, 144, 148
Li Shang-yin, 86
Lin-chi Sect, 21, 49, 71
Ling-yu, 41
Liu Ch'iu, 32
Liu K'o-chuang, 57, 71
Lo Ta-ching, 76, 80
Lotus Sutra, 64, 117, 121, 122
Lü Pen-chung, 40, 57, 58, 68, 71
Lu T'ung, 106
Lu Yu, 15, 16, 49, 76

Ma Lin, 105
Ma-Hsia School, 109–11, 114, 115, 123,
    124
Ma Yüan, 109, 110, 117
Madhyamaka-śāstra, 58
Mahākāśyapa, 43, 48
Manjuśrī, 34
Mei Yao-ch'en, 44, 86, 136
Mencius, 87
Meng Chia, 60
Meng Chiao, 139, 143
Meng Hao-jan, 53
Mu-chou, 41

Nāgārjuna, 58–59
Nan-ch'üan, 50, 62

Ou-yang Hsiu, 44, 136

Pai-chang, 41
Pañca-vimśati-sāhāsrikā-prajñā-pāramitā-
    sūtra, 79
P'ang Yün, 50
Pao-p'u-tzu, 123
Pass Without a Gate (Wu-men kuan), 38,
    43, 45, 50, 62, 74
Pi-yen lu, 38

Po Chü-yi, 50, 69, 75, 95–98, 136
P'u-hua, 72

Ssu-k'ung T'u, 46–47
Ssu-ma Ch'ien, 47
Su Shih, 39, 46, 47, 53, 61, 62, 76, 109,
    136–39, 141, 143
Su Wu, 50, 54
Sung-shih ch'ao, 74

Ta-chih-tu lun, 79
Ta-yü, 49
T'ao Ch'ien (Yüan-ming), 44, 84, 87, 97,
    102, 103, 118, 144
Tao-te ching, 87, 117
Tao-ying, 48
Tseng Chi, 71
Ts'ui Po, 131
Tu Fu, 26, 44, 47, 53, 54, 60–62, 69, 76,
    84, 86, 95, 96, 126, 142

Vimalakīrti, 28, 33, 34

Wang An-shih, 40, 41, 44, 53, 76, 141
Wang Hui-chih, 132
Wang Shou-jen, 147
Wang Wei, 103, 124
Wen T'ung, 132
Wen-yen, 41
Wu K'o, 40
Wu Ti, 79

Yang Chang-ju, 46, 49
Yang Wan-li: at court, 24, 29–32; death,
    36; early official career, 16–19;
    meeting with Chang Chün, 18–19;
    mission to Chin, 31–32; retirement,
    33–36; service in Kuangtung, 28–29;
    sudden enlightenment, 26–27

WORKS — POETRY:
"After a Rain, I Get up at Dawn to
    Look at the Mountains," 118
"After a relapse of bladder di-
    sease. . . . ," 33
"Approaching Holidays," 28
"As I Cook Breakfast at New Grove, I
    Gaze on Bell Mountain," 110
"As my Boat Passes Goose Walk River

Mouth, I Gaze at Chicken Coop Mountain in Ho-chou," 110

"At Morning I Set Out From *Dharma* Enlightenment Monastery . . . ," 128

"Ballad of Hsi-E, The," 101–102

"Because of my Aging Eyes I Sigh as I Give up Books," 22

"Boat Passes An-jen, The," 114

"Boat People, The," 97

"Boatman Plays a Flute, The," 70

"Bubbles," 83

"Chanting Bitterly," 106–107

"Chanting While Drunk," 94

"Clearing Snow," 64

"Cooking Breakfast at Jade Field, I Hear an Oriole and See a Stork," 128–29

"Crossing Flower Bridge at Dawn, I Enter the Boundary of Hsüan-chou," 114

"Crossing the Yangtze River," 31–32

"Day after the *Shang-ssu* Festival I stroll in the East Garden with Tzu-wen, Po-chung, and Yung-nien, The," 133

"Don't Read Books," 91

"Drinking Late," 26

"Entering the Boundary of Floating Beam," 140

"Freezing Fly, The," 130

"Garden of Youth," 87

"Gazing at Li Po's Grave on the Hsieh Family's Green Mountain," 94

"Gazing from Lichee Hall During the Evening," 89

"Getting Up Early on an Autumn Day," 81

"Herding Boys at An-le Fang," 101

"I Break Out in Song While Spending the Night at East Bank," 119

"I Enter the East Ministry Early in the Morning When the Waning Moon Has Just Risen," 112–13

"I Follow Behind Uncle Ch'ang-ying to Go out Visiting on 'Man' Day at Dawn," 73

"I Gaze at the Moon on a Frosty Night from my Study 'Snow Angling Boat,' " 60

"I Make Fun of a Little Boy," 88

"I receive a letter from my two sons. . . . ," 85

"I Set off at Morning from Rush Field and am Moved When I See an Egret," 127

"I Sing of a Bamboo Grove . . . ," 132

"I Sleep Exhausted at Snow Angling Boat," 25

"I Thank the Tea Secretary of Chien-chou . . . ," 89

"I Wash My Face, a Short Poem," 145

"I Write What I Saw in Jest," 131

"In Answer to Chung-liang's Extemporaneous Poem on the End of Spring," 90

"In Answer to Li T'ien-lin," 41–42

"In Late Spring I Walk in the Fields at South Flats," 97–98

"In the Evening Heat I Roam by a Lotus Pond," 133–34

"In the Morning I Leave the Prefectural City . . . ," 139–40

"Inns by the Side of the Road," 99

"Later Song About Suffering from the Cold, A," 107

"Light Rain," 59

"Looking at the Snow on a Moon-lit Night," 66

"Making Fire in the Boat on a Snowy Day," 63

"Morning was bright and clear. . . . ," 120

"Moved by Autumn," 143–44, 145

"Night Rain," 136–37

"On Hearing the Wind's Sound at Night," 74

"On Leaving the River Mouth at Cross Mountain," 94–95

"On the Eighth of the Fourth Month I Eat New Lichees," 28

"On the Fifth of the Fifth Month I Stop Drinking Due to Illness," 75

"On the Thirteenth of the Fourth Month I Cross Lake Po-yang," 104

"On the Night of the Twelfth of the Eighth Month I Gaze at the Moon from Sincere Study," 65

"On the Road to Wan-ling," 116

"On the Third Day of the First Month

I spend the Night at the Fan Clan Village," 93
"Pair of Pagodas at Orchid Creek, A," 118–19
"Passing Hsieh Family Bay," 115
"Passing West Mountain," 22–23
"Passing White Sand, a Bamboo Branch Song," 96
"Picking a Plum with Snow under Candlelight," 134
"Planting Rice Song," 100–101
"Playing with the Moon on a Summer Night," 78
"Raven, The," 129
"Reading Books," 25
"Realm of Idleness, The," 34
"Returning Home Drunk the Next Day," 92
"Riding a Boat Outside Heaven Gate," 142, 144
"River Water," 64
"Sending off Tseng Wu-yi to Become a Historian," 30
"Setting off at Silver Tree Grove," 117
"Song of the Water Mantis, The," 127
"Spending the Night at the River-Port Pool Rock," 71
"Spring Cold," 116
"Suffering from the Cold," 108
"Two Days After Double Nine . . . ," 80
"Watching a Children's Festival for Welcoming a God," 86
"Watching a Small Boy Play at Beating the Spring Ox," 100

"Watching Ants," 128
"Watching Fish," 130–131
"Watching the Planting," 99
"Watching the Rain," 138
"Watering a Pot of Calamus and Narcissus Flowers," 33
"When my term as Governor of Ling-ling has finished . . . . ," 85
"When Tz'u-kung's period of service is completed . . . . ," 86
"While ill, my feet start hurting again. . . . ," 34
"Written in Jest," 93
"Written on the Wang Family Inn at Green Mountain Market," 132–33
"Written While on the Road to Wan-an," 66

WORKS — PROSE:
Poetry Talks, 60, 61, 69
Policy of a Thousand Precautions, 23–24
Preface to Ch'ao-t'ien chi, 49–50
Preface to Nan-hai chi, 45–46, 48–49

Yeh Hsieh, 50, 55
Yen Yü, 52–55
Yi-hsüan, 49, 72
Yoshikawa Kōjirō, 95, 136
Yu Mou, 46, 50, 99
Yüan Chen, 50
Yüan Hung-tao, 147
Yüan Mei, 148–49
Yüeh Fei, 17–18, 32

PL2687
·Y3
Z87

770709

A000002375489